Teacher's Guide

John Jackman Wendy Wren

Published in 2001 by:
Nelson Thornes Ltd
Delta Place
27 Bath Road
CHELTENHAM
GL53 7TH
United Kingdom

01 02 03 04 05 / 10 9 8 7 6 5 4 3 2 1

A catalogue record for this book is available from the British Library

ISBN 0-17-424802-4

Page make-up by Clive Sutherland

Printed and bound in Croatia by Zrinski

Contents

General Introduction

The teaching of literacy and English in schools

Children can become fully and effectively literate only if they are given both the opportunity to communicate and the skills to support such communication. This view, which represents the deeply-held belief of many teachers and is embraced by a large majority of UK primary schools, is now embodied in the National Literacy Strategy and the National Curriculum for England, as well as the Scottish National Guidelines for English Language 5–14, the Northern Ireland Curriculum Orders and Wales Curriculum 2000. As a result, and particularly since the implementation of the National Literacy Strategy (NLS) in England, there has been an improvement in reading skills amongst primary school children. However, test results for writing lag well behind, indicating that this area needs special attention. The areas of concern are as follows.

- Non-fiction writing skills have been identified as being in particular need of improvement.
- Poor spelling skills indicate inadequate knowledge of spelling rules and conventions.
- Sentence construction and punctuation are weak.
- There is an apparent lack of planning, reviewing and editing skills.

Some of these weaknesses result from children having had insufficient text 'models' from which to work.

Introducing *Nelson English*

Nelson English is a clearly structured and rigorous skills-based course that aims to improve pupils' understanding and use of the written word. The 1994 edition quickly became well established in schools throughout the UK and overseas as an English course that focused particularly on raising standards in children's writing. It was noted for its 'twin-track' structure, which focused separately on the basic 'skills' of the English language (punctuation, grammar, spelling, etc.) and their 'development' within the context of comprehension and writing. It was also noted for its 'spiral' curriculum, which is now reflected in the National Literacy Strategy *Framework for Teaching*.

This edition of *Nelson English* builds on the underlying philosophy and key benefits of the 1994 edition in the following ways.

- Each unit contains a stimulus passage.
- Comprehension activities collectively seek to elicit literal, inferential, deductive and evaluative responses.
- The basic skills of vocabulary, spelling, grammar and punctuation or sentence construction are covered in each unit, where possible in the context of the passage stimulus.

- Each unit concludes with a writing activity modelled on or developed from the stimulus passage.

The course, therefore, continues to support existing good practice in schools, helping to meet all the current concerns about standards in writing.

The Key Stage 1 material comes in three levels:

- Blue Level for Reception
- Red Level for Year 1
- Yellow Level for Year 2.

All levels provide structured, full-colour material for each year group, for use with support and guidance from the teacher. The scheme is compact in its presentation, comprising a deliberately limited number of components – described on pages 7 to 15 – making for ease of classroom use. You will quickly find your way around the scheme, and your pupils will appreciate the accessible and inviting layout of the **posters** and **pupil's books**.

Welcome to the New Edition

The new edition retains the same winning formula of skills and development work, integrating them into the new twin tracks of Fiction and Non-fiction. This approach aids the effective teaching of the different skills required for writing in these two distinct contexts. As a result, children's skills as they are applied to writing both fiction and non-fiction will improve, and giving equal weight to non-fiction work will help to maintain the interest level of boys in particular. The fiction and non-fiction tracks also have the advantage of mirroring the National Literacy Strategy objectives for the text level work.

An important feature of the new edition is the separate **Copymaster Resource Book**, which contains Comprehension, Word skills and Writing copymasters for each unit. At Foundation and Year 1, the **Copymaster Resource Book** provides all of the writing component of the course, whilst at Year 2 it supports the writing tasks found in the **pupil's books**.

Nelson English uses these new features, together with the proven strengths of the 1994 edition, to support you in the classroom. It ensures that you cover the basics of the core curriculum, fundamental not only to the National Literacy Strategy and the National Curriculum for England, but also the Scottish National Guidelines for English Language 5–14, the Northern Ireland Curriculum Orders and Wales Curriculum 2000. The links to each of these curricula are clearly shown in the accompanying **Correlation Guide**. Please note that, where curricular requirements differ, *Nelson English* errs in favour of introducing new concepts sooner rather than later.

How to use *Nelson English*

Using *Nelson English* at Red Level

The fiction and non-fiction twin tracks cover a wide range of genres, with the fiction track incorporating poetry. Together, the two tracks cover the core curriculum for Year One classes, parallel units being thematically linked. To ensure progressive coverage of all the necessary skills, we strongly recommend that you work through the units in order and that you complete the parallel units from both tracks before you move on to the next. Whilst each unit is designed to stand alone, new concepts are often first introduced in the fiction track. We therefore suggest that you work through the fiction unit before the parallel non-fiction unit.

This **Teacher's Guide** provides teaching notes for each unit. We recommend that you read the teaching notes before you begin working on a particular unit with your class. New concepts are introduced slowly and ample opportunity is given for consolidation. It is never assumed that a skill will be mastered immediately. We have been careful to present material that is accessible to the majority of pupils, but believe that – within their individual limitations – most children prefer to be stretched.

Every unit is supported by Comprehension, Word skills and Writing copymasters, all contained in the **Copymaster Resource Book**. These may be used for a variety of purposes, including consolidation, differentiation and extension, and are cross-referenced in the **Teacher's Guide**.

Nelson English

Blue Level
4–5 years

Poster pack
ISBN 0-17-424801-6

Copymaster Resource Book
ISBN 0-17-424800-8

Teacher's Guide
ISBN 0-17-424799-0

Red Level
5–6 years

Poster pack
ISBN 0-17-424803-2

Beginning Fiction Skills
ISBN 0-17-424804-0

Beginning Non-fiction Skills
ISBN 0-17-424805-9

Copymaster Resource Book
ISBN 0-17-424813-X

Fiction Workbook
ISBN 0-17-424806-7 (x10)

Non-fiction Workbook
ISBN 0-17-424807-5 (x10)

Teacher's Guide
ISBN 0-17-424802-4

Yellow Level
6–7 years

Poster pack
ISBN 0-17-424810-5

Beginning Fiction Skills
ISBN 0-17-424811-3

Beginning Non-fiction Skills
ISBN 0-17-424812-1

Copymaster Resource Book
ISBN 0-17-424809-1

Teacher's Guide
ISBN 0-17-424808-3

Components of Red Level

Posters and Pupil's Books

At Red Level, there are 18 units of work – 9 fiction and 9 non-fiction. Each unit is based on stimulus material presented on the poster and in the pupil's book. Each fiction and non-fiction unit poster, which introduces the unit theme, leads into the relevant pupil's book unit. These stimulus texts are presented in a variety of styles and typefaces and cover the required reading range for Year 1.

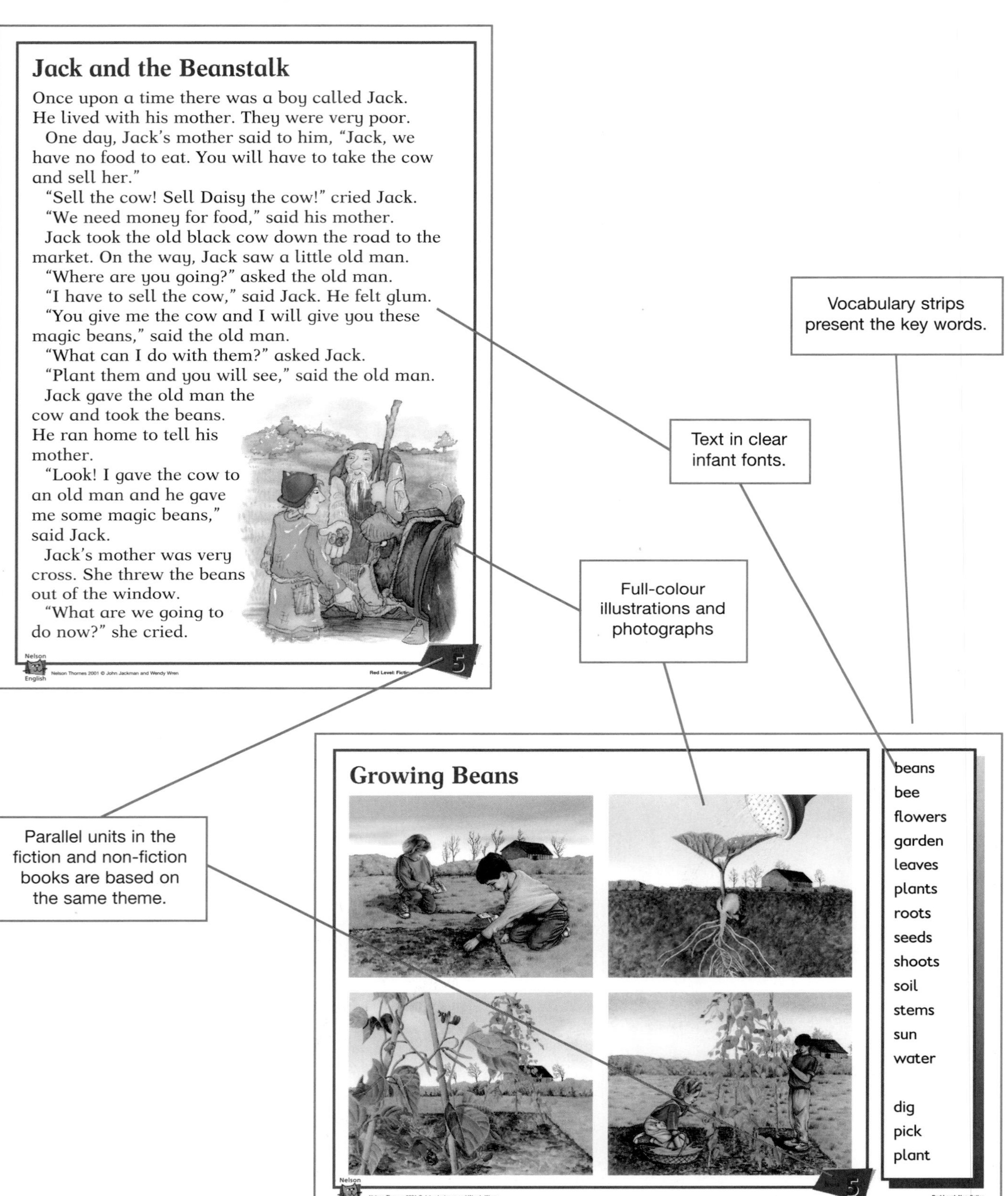

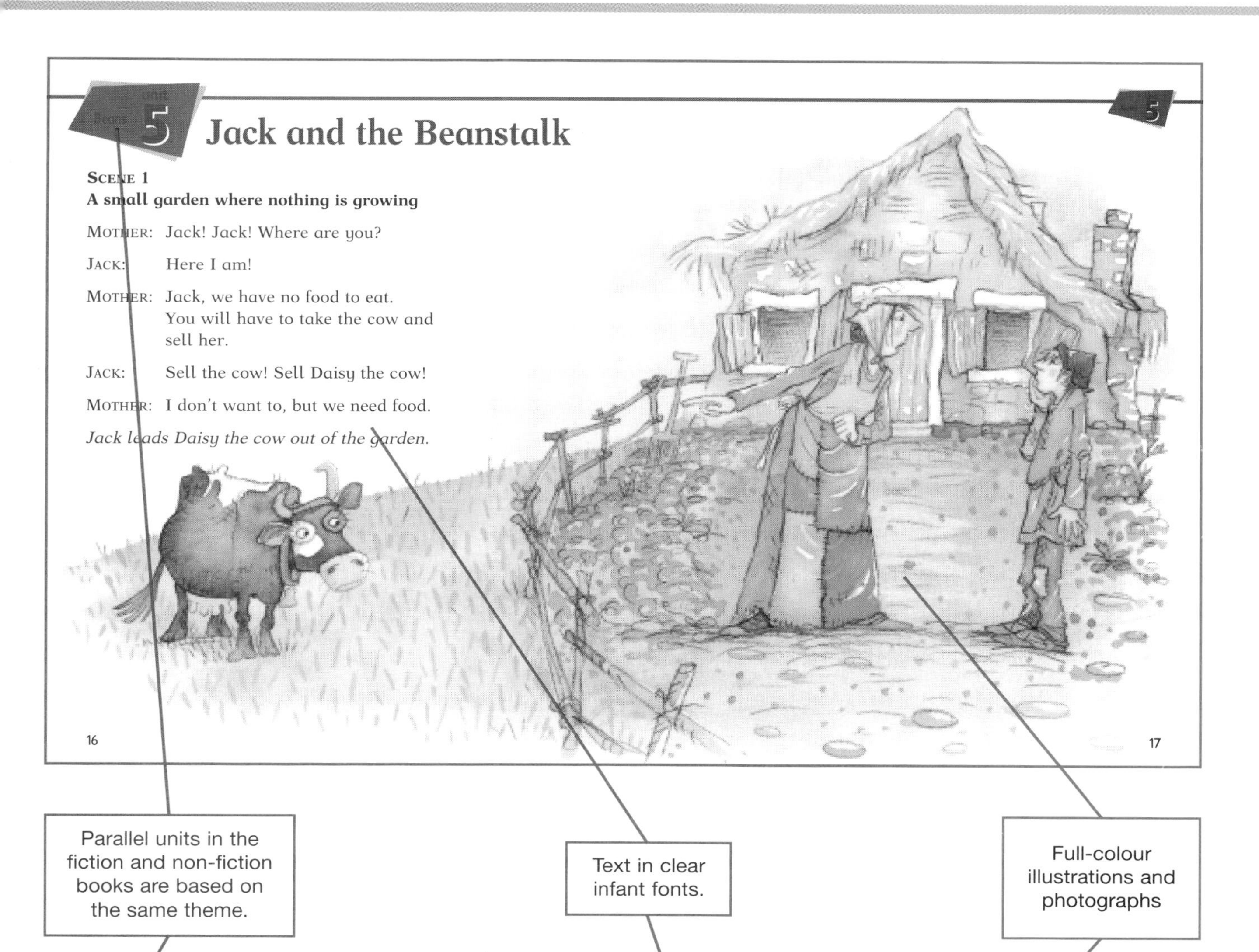

unit 5 Beans

Jack and the Beanstalk

Scene 1
A small garden where nothing is growing

Mother: Jack! Jack! Where are you?

Jack: Here I am!

Mother: Jack, we have no food to eat. You will have to take the cow and sell her.

Jack: Sell the cow! Sell Daisy the cow!

Mother: I don't want to, but we need food.

Jack leads Daisy the cow out of the garden.

16 17

Parallel units in the fiction and non-fiction books are based on the same theme.

Text in clear infant fonts.

Full-colour illustrations and photographs

unit 5 Beans

Growing Beans

18 19

Teacher's Guide

In this **Teacher's Guide**, each unit opens with a 'reading range' statement and a box that summarises the NLS objectives covered in the unit. Also listed, but displayed in italics and marked with a 'triangle' symbol, are any teaching objectives that are not taken from the relevant term's NLS objectives. These items give you the opportunity to revise points already covered or to anticipate additional areas of work that are relevant to the topics being taught.

The NLS box is followed by an introductory section providing suggestions for initial class text work and teaching ideas to support group and independent work. These detailed notes focus on text-, word- and sentence-level objectives in turn. Text-level work is returned to at the end of the teaching notes, where the focus is on writing.

The Comprehension, Word skills and Writing copymasters are referred to, and suggestions are made for their use.

At the end of each unit section in the **Teacher's Guide** are answers for the copymasters, together with facsimiles of that unit's poster and copymasters for easy reference.

A Scope and Sequence Chart (pages 18-21) summarises the educational content of the course for the whole year.

A separate **Correlation Guide** correlates the whole of *Nelson English* to the National Curriculum for England. **Correlation Guides** are also available for matching *Nelson English* to the curricula for Scotland, Northern Ireland and Wales.

The NLS box quotes from those NLS objectives that are met (either fully or in part) within the unit.

Toys & In the Park

Non-fiction

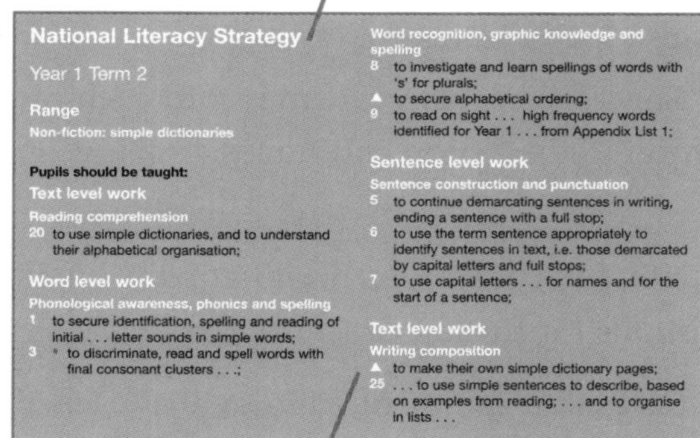

National Literacy Strategy

Year 1 Term 2

Range

Non-fiction: simple dictionaries

Pupils should be taught:

Text level work

Reading comprehension

20 to use simple dictionaries, and to understand their alphabetical organisation;

Word level work

Phonological awareness, phonics and spelling

1 to secure identification, spelling and reading of initial . . . letter sounds in simple words;

3 * to discriminate, read and spell words with final consonant clusters . . .;

Word recognition, graphic knowledge and spelling

8 to investigate and learn spellings of words with 's' for plurals;

▲ to secure alphabetical ordering;

9 to read on sight . . . high frequency words identified for Year 1 . . . from Appendix List 1;

Sentence level work

Sentence construction and punctuation

5 to continue demarcating sentences in writing, ending a sentence with a full stop;

6 to use the term sentence appropriately to identify sentences in text, i.e. those demarcated by capital letters and full stops;

7 to use capital letters . . . for names and for the start of a sentence;

Text level work

Writing composition

▲ to make their own simple dictionary pages;

25 . . . to use simple sentences to describe, based on examples from reading; . . . and to organise in lists . . .

Teaching Notes

Poster: Shared reading

Text level work

Introduce the subject of toys and ask questions such as:

- What is your favourite toy?
- Which toy have you had the longest?
- What is the newest toy you have?

Display the poster and discuss with the children what they can see in the picture. Ask them to say what toys the children are playing with (i.e. skateboard, boat, ball, frisby, bat and ball, kite, roller skates, etc.); point to the words they use on the vocabulary strip. Can they spot the game the children are playing which requires no toy (hide and seek)? Do the children have a park near where they live? Do they play in the park? What sort of games do they play? Do they take toys to

The first list on the vocabulary strip is the names of the main objects in the picture. Read through the object words with the children and ask if they notice anything about the list (i.e. it is in alphabetical order). The second list on the vocabulary strip deals with action words (see Word level work).

Suggest the names of other toys not pictured on the poster. Invite individuals to come forward and indicate where on the vocabulary list each word would go, depending on its initial letter. Avoid suggesting toys with the same initial letter as those already on the list as, at this stage, alphabetical ordering need only be by first letter.

Word level work

Refresh the children's memories about '-ng' words, which can be separated into two main categories: those in which '-ng' is a phoneme within the root word, e.g. *bang*, and those in which '-ng' is part of a suffix, e.g. *playing*. In both cases, help the children to hear the nasal 'ng' sound.

Given that 'ing' is used to form the present continuous tense (e.g. *He is playing*.), ask volunteers to suggest sentences about what is happening in the picture on the poster. When they refer to the actions listed in the vocabulary strip, point this out. Encourage the class to note that these words all end in 'ing'.

See whether anyone can suggest action words (verbs) other than those listed and, if so, make a list of these on the board. Ask the children to copy some of the 'ing' words, drawing a small picture next to each to indicate they are aware of its meaning.

Play a word game with different children miming an action at your suggestion (e.g. *digging, hopping, jumping, shouting*). The others guess what they are doing, giving their answers using an 'ing' word.

Use **Word Skills Copymaster 6 Non-fiction** for support with 'ing' words.

Sentence level work

Acting as scribe, ask the children to dictate a sentence about the poster. Write it without the initial capital letter and full stop. Invite suggestions about what mistakes you have made. If appropriate, invite a volunteer to correct your errors. Invite suggestions for another sentence. This time, write it correctly, and invite a child to circle the two things (capital letter and full stop) that show it is a sentence.

Pupil's book

Text level work

Introduction

Following on from the poster work, the pupil's book shows two pages of a simple picture dictionary which continues the theme of toys.

Discuss the pages with the children, leading them to understand that each dictionary entry has a word that is the name of a toy, an explanation of the word (definition), an illustration of the object, and that the words are arranged in alphabetical order.

Ask the children to suggest names of other toys. Make a list on the board and encourage them to say where on the dictionary pages each new word would go, e.g. *roller-skates* would go after *kite* and before *skipping-rope*. The children may suggest words with the same letters as words in the pupil's book. Explain alphabetical ordering by second and third letters, so the children realise there is a mechanism for doing so, even though this work is not tackled until later in the course.

Reading comprehension

In section A of **Comprehension Copymaster 6 Non-fiction** children are required to answer questions establishing literal comprehension of the passage in the pupil's book. Section B provides practice in alphabetical ordering. Section A can be approached as a class discussion, in guided or independently working groups, or individually.

Word level work

Important words

Use various alphabet charts, if available, to establish the concept of simple (first letter) alphabetical ordering. Discuss why ordering items in this way can be helpful, perhaps using simple reference books and dictionaries to demonstrate, emphasising that if things were arranged randomly in such books it would be much more difficult to find them.

Teach the children an alphabet song to help them to begin to remember the order of letters in the alphabet.

Remind the children that letters have names as well as sounds, and ensure everyone is familiar and confident in recognising both.

Ask individual children, pairs or groups to copy the letters of the alphabet down the left-hand side of a sheet of paper. Next to each letter, ask the children to write the name of an object (e.g. a toy) beginning with that letter. Spelling may cause some problems but, for the purpose of this activity, the most important aspect is that the initial letters are correct.

This activity can be repeated using different categories (e.g. household/classroom objects, foods, etc.) or practised verbally, in the form of the memory game 'I went to market and I bought . . .', with each child adding an item beginning with the next letter of the alphabet.

The high-frequency words for this unit, to be taught as 'sight recognition' words, are as follows.

boy
girl
house
home
little

Sentence level work

Sentences and capital letters

Having discussed toys and games, ask a child to say what is their favourite toy. Write on the board (for example): *The toy Alice likes best is her Barbie.* Point out that the initial letter of a person's name is always a capital (or upper case) letter. Ask each child to write a similar sentence about their neighbour's favourite toys or games.

Remind them that their sentence must begin with a capital (upper case) letter and finish with a full stop, and that names must also begin with capital (upper case) letters.

The unit markers, indexed down the side of the page, enable you to turn rapidly to the appropriate section of the Guide.

Objectives marked '▲' are additional items, not taken from this term's NLS objectives.

NLS Appendix List 1 of high-frequency words has been divided between the units, so each unit targets five of the words for pupils to learn.

Text level work

Writing composition

Writing Copymaster 6 Non-fiction requires children to put into alphabetical order some simple sight vocabulary. The copymaster includes the alphabet, to provide support for children who are still unsure of alphabetical order. For children who can cope without having the alphabet written out for reference, cover or ink it out on the copymaster.

If possible, let the children work in pairs/groups and make their own simple picture dictionaries connected to topic work, e.g. animals. Explain that there will be three stages for each word:

1 write the word
2 draw a picture to illustrate the word
3 write an explanation (definition) of the word.

Use one sheet of paper for each word and give each group of children a different set of letters to work on, so that the finished class work can be displayed in alphabetical order, as a complete dictionary.

Copymaster answers

Comprehension Copymaster 6

A 1 doll
2 cuddly toy
3 kite
4 kite

B 1 'Crayons' would come after ball and before doll.
2 'Football' would come after doll and before kite.
3 'Yo-yo' would come after teddy bear.

Word Skills Copymaster 6

1 Simon is kicking the ball.
2 The dog is chasing the ball.
3 Indira is flying her new kite.
4 Lenny is throwing the frisbee.
5 Lara is riding her bike.
6 The baby is digging in the sand.

Writing Copymaster 6

and
boy
cat
for
go
he
is
look
mum
on
play
saw
tree
up
we
you

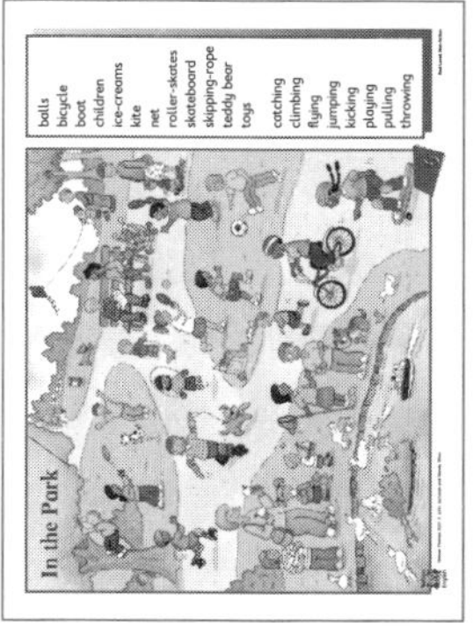

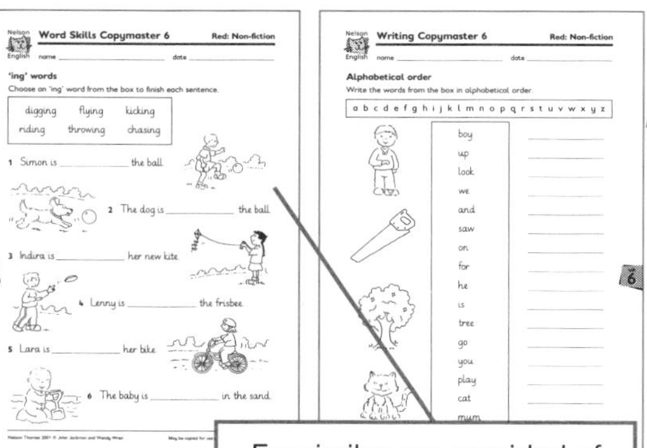

Answers are supplied for the copymasters.

Facsimiles are provided of the poster and copymasters for the relevant unit.

68

Copymaster Resource Book

The copymasters in the **Copymaster Resource Book**, linked to the texts in the **pupil's books** and **posters**, may be used for consolidation, differentiation and extension. Three copymasters are supplied for each unit, as follows:

- Comprehension copymaster
- Word skills copymaster
- Writing copymaster.

The **Copymaster Resource Book** also includes the following:

- a photocopiable Pupil Record Sheet, on which you can record each pupil's progress as he or she works through the fiction and non-fiction copymasters;
- photocopiable spelling lists relating to each unit's high-frequency words, which can be taken home by pupils for further practice;
- a Look-say-cover-write-check Sheet that can be filled in by the teacher with words appropriate to each pupil's ability.

Workbooks

The Comprehension, Word skills and Writing copymasters are also available as a collection within the Fiction and Non-fiction Workbooks. These enable each individual child's work to be kept together for ease and convenience.

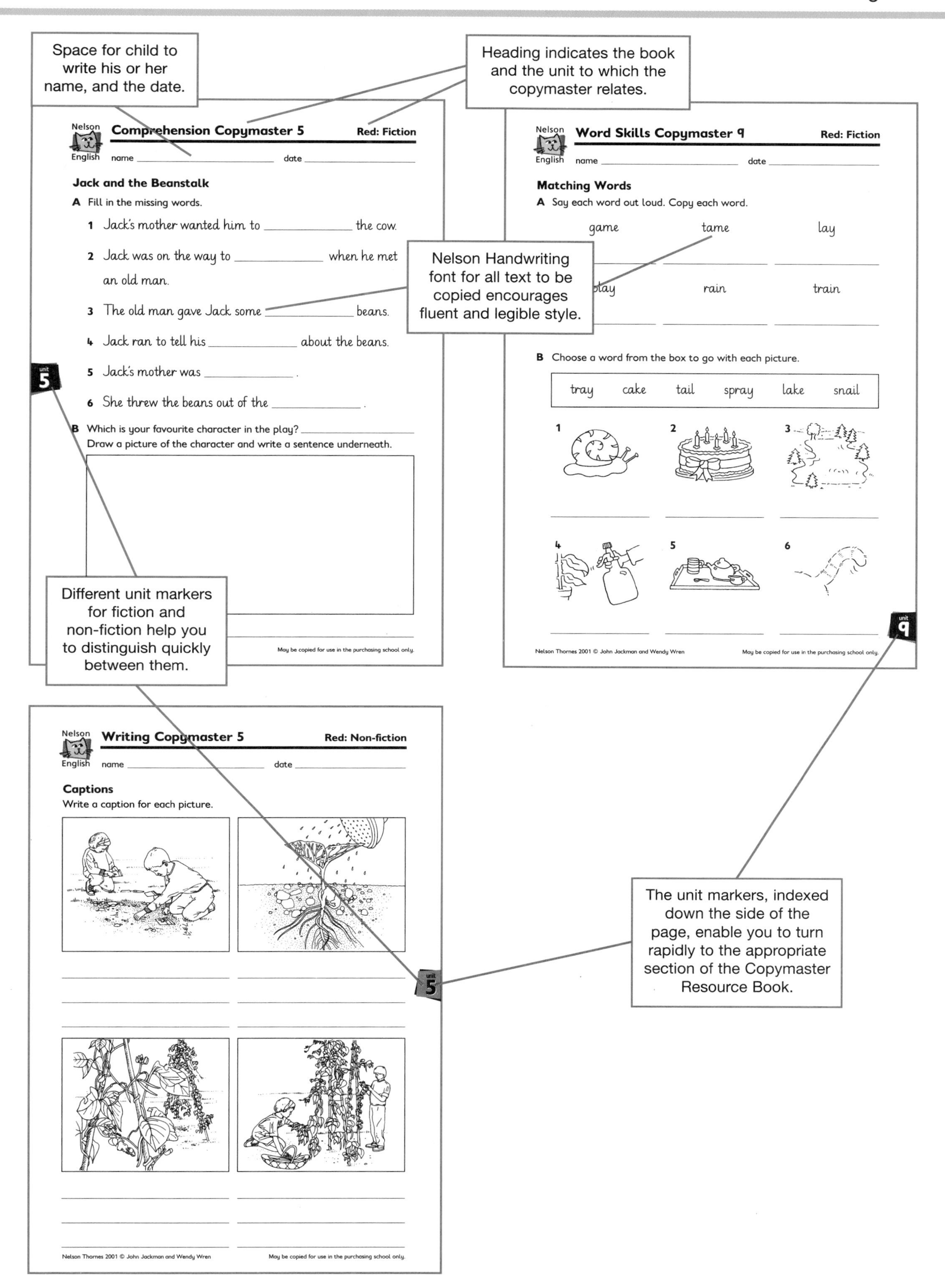
Space for child to write his or her name, and the date.
Heading indicates the book and the unit to which the copymaster relates.
Nelson English
Comprehension Copymaster 5
Red: Fiction
name
date
Jack and the Beanstalk
A Fill in the missing words.
1 Jack's mother wanted him to ______ the cow.
2 Jack was on the way to ______ when he met an old man.
3 The old man gave Jack some ______ beans.
4 Jack ran to tell his ______ about the beans.
5 Jack's mother was ______.
6 She threw the beans out of the ______.
B Which is your favourite character in the play?
Draw a picture of the character and write a sentence underneath.
May be copied for use in the purchasing school only.
unit 5
Word Skills Copymaster 9
Red: Fiction
Matching Words
A Say each word out loud. Copy each word.
game
tame
lay
play
rain
train
Nelson Handwriting font for all text to be copied encourages fluent and legible style.
B Choose a word from the box to go with each picture.
tray
cake
tail
spray
lake
snail
Nelson Thornes 2001 © John Jackman and Wendy Wren
May be copied for use in the purchasing school only.
unit 9
Different unit markers for fiction and non-fiction help you to distinguish quickly between them.
Writing Copymaster 5
Red: Non-fiction
Captions
Write a caption for each picture.
Nelson Thornes 2001 © John Jackman and Wendy Wren
May be copied for use in the purchasing school only.
unit 5
The unit markers, indexed down the side of the page, enable you to turn rapidly to the appropriate section of the Copymaster Resource Book.

Look-say-cover-write-check

'Look, say, cover, write, check' is a well-tried and effective device to help with the memorising of individual words and groups of words, which has now both proved itself and been recommended in a number of National Curriculum documents. The Look-say-cover-write-check Sheet supplied in the **Copymaster Resource Book** can be filled in with either the high frequency words to be covered in that unit or other words appropriate to the ability of the individual child. The words for the child to learn should be written in the boxes on the left-hand side. There are then four further boxes going across the sheet, in which the child can practise spelling each word. The child should be encouraged to:

- look carefully at the letters in each word
- say the word quietly to themselves
- cover the word, either with their hand or by folding the sheet of paper over
- write the word
- check back to see if they spelt it correctly.

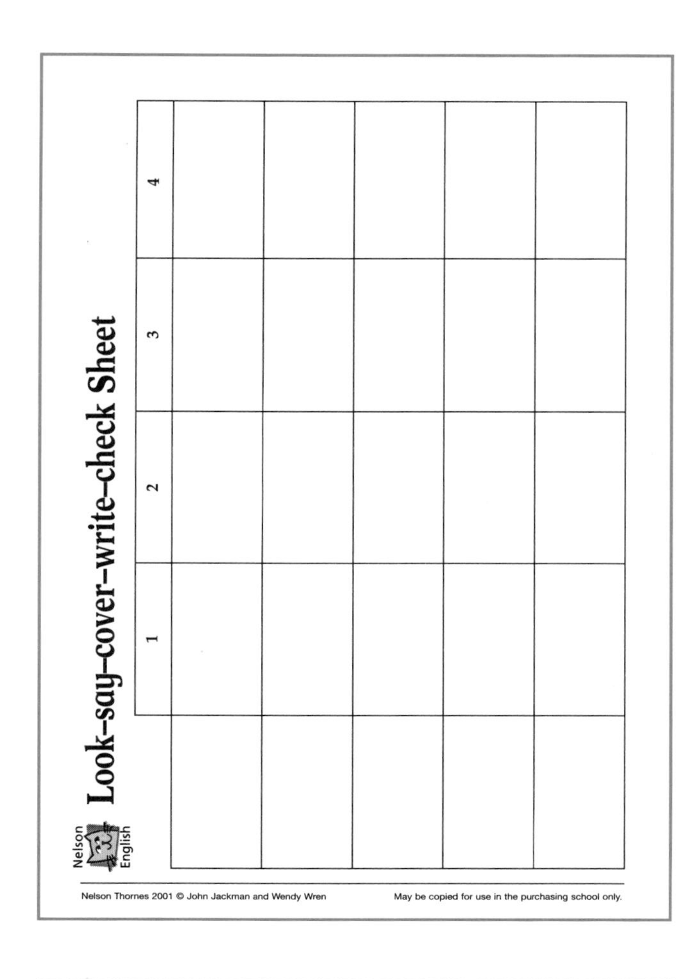

Nelson English

Look–say–cover–write–check Sheet

	1	2	3	4

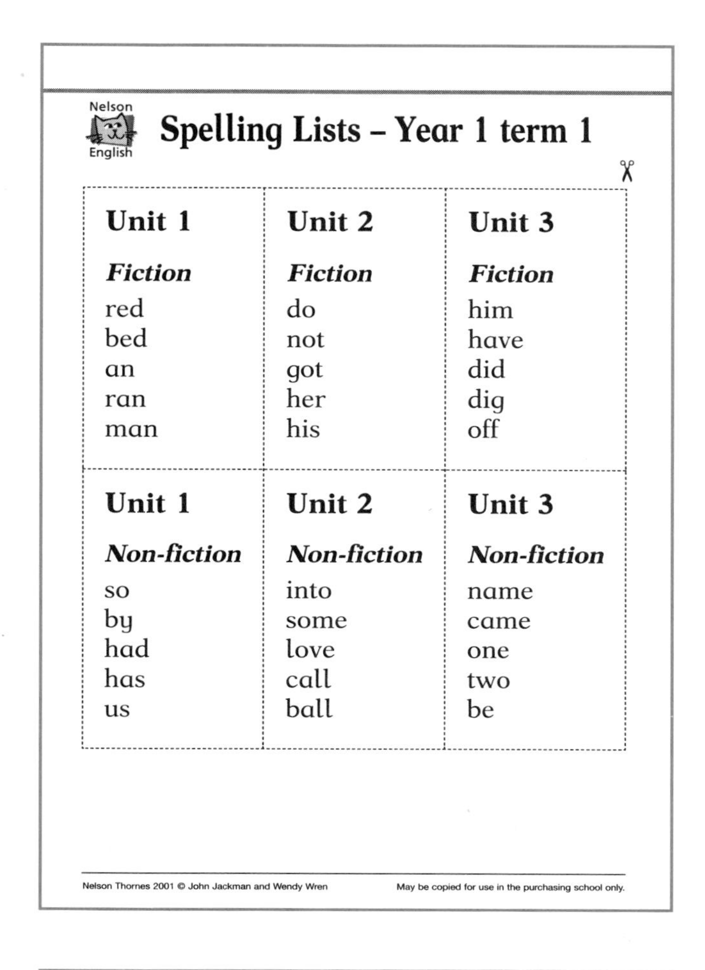

Nelson English

Spelling Lists – Year 1 term 1

Unit 1 *Fiction*	Unit 2 *Fiction*	Unit 3 *Fiction*
red	do	him
bed	not	have
an	got	did
ran	her	dig
man	his	off

Unit 1 *Non-fiction*	Unit 2 *Non-fiction*	Unit 3 *Non-fiction*
so	into	name
by	some	came
had	love	one
has	call	two
us	ball	be

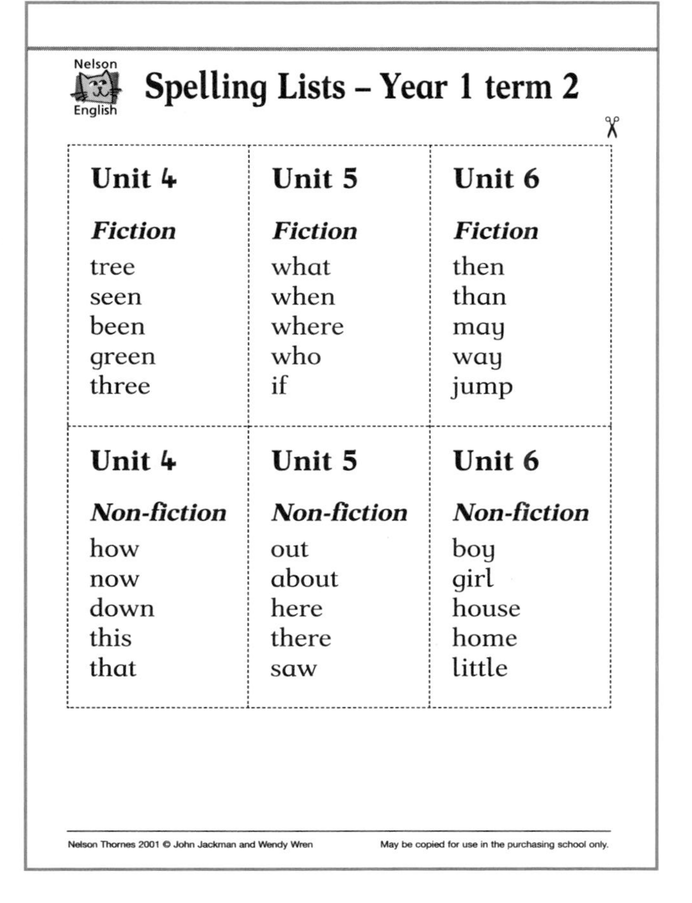

Nelson English

Spelling Lists – Year 1 term 2

Unit 4 *Fiction*	Unit 5 *Fiction*	Unit 6 *Fiction*
tree	what	then
seen	when	than
been	where	may
green	who	way
three	if	jump

Unit 4 *Non-fiction*	Unit 5 *Non-fiction*	Unit 6 *Non-fiction*
how	out	boy
now	about	girl
down	here	house
this	there	home
that	saw	little

Nelson English

Spelling Lists – Year 1 term 3

Unit 7 *Fiction*	Unit 8 *Fiction*	Unit 9 *Fiction*
can't	four	Monday
don't	five	Tuesday
good	six	Wednesday
from	seven	Thursday
as	blue	Friday

Unit 7 *Non-fiction*	Unit 8 *Non-fiction*	Unit 9 *Non-fiction*
our	eight	Saturday
your	nine	Sunday
back	ten	brown
help	yellow	pink
will	black	white

Classroom Management

Nelson English and the Literacy Hour

Nelson English is designed to facilitate the Literacy Hour, but is not to be seen as a straitjacket. It both acknowledges the flexibility intended when the NLS was constructed and seeks to encourage the natural desire of many teachers to bring their own interpretation and knowledge to their English teaching. *Nelson English* recognises the importance of the teacher being able to approach a unit of work and decide, depending on circumstances, which sections are undertaken as whole-class, group or independent work.

You can feel confident that, by following the course sequentially, you will have covered the essentials of the writing strategy.

Timing

The timing of activities within the Literacy Hour is often discussed, but we believe that it is only the teacher who, within the context of the class, can make specific timing decisions. Furthermore, many of the activities, especially the writing activities, quite properly require an allocation of time over and above the Literacy Hour.

Nelson English and the National Curriculum for England

Nelson English rigorously covers the writing requirements in each national curriculum, including those contained within the National Curriculum for England, which states:

> During Key Stage 1, pupils start to enjoy writing and see the value of it. They learn to communicate meaning in narrative and non-fiction texts and spell and punctuate correctly.

Nelson English is based on this definition of the writing skills that pupils should develop between the ages of five and seven, which it covers thoroughly. For further details, please see the separate **Correlation Guide**.

Note that, whilst planning, drafting and editing are not always explicit requirements of the activities at Key Stage 1, it is recommended that these skills are introduced gradually so pupils see them as an integral part of the writing process.

Although the main focus of *Nelson English* is on writing, it also embraces many of the other literacy objectives, including speaking and listening skills, either directly through activities in the **pupil's books**, or by way of suggestions in the **Teacher's Guides**. The resulting programme provides a well-balanced curriculum, enabling your pupils to maximise their achievement in the end-of-Key-Stage assessments.

Differentiation

Differentiation is built into the copymaster activities either by a gradual increase in difficulty, as in the case of the comprehension questions, or, in other activities, by using the device of lettered blocks of questions of increasing difficulty.

Handwriting

Handwriting skills are not covered specifically by *Nelson English*. However, the course indirectly encourages pupils to develop a fluent and legible style by using the *Nelson Handwriting* font, the most popular handwriting style in UK schools, which follows the NLS implicitly. The font is used for most of the copymaster activities that require children to copy from the text.

Scope and Sequence — RED LEVEL BEGINNING FICTION SKILLS

	Reading Comprehension	Phonics & Spelling
Unit 1 Holidays Little Bean	Make correspondence between words said and read Discuss story settings and relate to own experience	Secure alphabetic letter knowledge Secure ability to hear initial and final phonemes in cvc words Discriminate and segment phonemes in cvc words
Unit 2 Birthdays Duncan's Tree House	Describe story settings and incidents Relate these to own experience	Discriminate and segment phonemes in cvc words Represent three phonemes in writing rhyming sets Learn new words from reading
Unit 3 Food 'Jelly on the Plate' and 'The Pancake'	Recite predictable rhymes Extend repeating patterns Substitute words and phrases	Recognise critical features of words – words within words Collect words related to topic
Unit 4 Foxes The Gingerbread Man	Re-tell stories, giving main points in sequence Discuss reasons for incidents in stories Identify and discuss characters	Investigate, read and spell words ending in ... *ff*, *ll*, *ss*, *ck*, *ng* Identify phonemes within words containing clusters
Unit 5 Beans Jack and the Beanstalk	Discuss characters' behaviour, appearance and qualities Become aware of character and dialogue Role-play parts in a play	Identify phonemes within words containing clusters Segment clusters into phonemes for writing
Unit 6 Toys Teddy Bear	Recite simple rhymes with actions Re-read them from the text	Recognise critical features of words – words within words Investigate spellings of words with 's' for plurals
Unit 7 Homes Hansel and Gretel & A strange House	Re-tell stories giving main points in sequence Pick out significant incidents Prepare and re-tell stories orally	Use the terms 'vowel' and 'consonant'
Unit 8 Tigers Mr Tig the Tiger	Re-tell stories giving main points in sequence Pick out significant incidents Compare and contrast stories with a variety of settings	Investigate and learn spellings of verbs with 'ed' and 'ing' endings
Unit 9 Myself 'Who Is It?', 'Everybody says' & 'After a Bath'	Read a variety of poems on similar themes Compare preferences Collect favourite poems	Explore common spelling patterns for long vowel phonemes Use the terms 'vowel' and 'consonant'

Grammar & Punctuation	Writing Composition	
Recognise whether captions and simple sentences make sense	Write about familiar incidents from story Make simple picture storybooks	**Unit 1 Holidays** Little Bean
Recognise full stops and capital letters Begin using the term *sentence* Understand that a line of writing is not the same as a sentence	Write about events in personal experience linked to incidents from story	**Unit 2 Birthdays** Duncan's Tree House
Name full stops and capital letters Understand that a line of writing is not the same as a sentence Understand that sentences need to make sense	Use rhymes as models for own writing	**Unit 3 Food** 'Jelly on the Plate' and 'The Pancake'
Predict words from preceding words in sentences Investigate words that 'fit' Suggest appropriate alternatives	Represent outlines of story plots Record main incidents in order Use elements of known stories to structure own writing	**Unit 4 Foxes** The Gingerbread Man
Demarcate sentences in writing with a capital letter and full stop Use the term *sentence* appropriately	Build simple profiles of characters	**Unit 5 Beans** Jack and the Beanstalk
Predict words from preceding words in sentence Investigate words that 'fit' Suggest appropriate alternatives Use capital letters for the personal pronoun 'I'	Substitute and extend rhyming patterns	**Unit 6 Toys** Teddy Bear
Explore word order by re-ordering sentences and discussing reasons why Reinforce knowledge of term *sentence*	Describe simple story settings	**Unit 7 Homes** Hansel and Gretel & A strange House
Identify common uses of capitalisation e.g. for personal titles, headings, emphasis Add question marks to questions Demarcate sentences in writing	Write about significant incidents from known stories	**Unit 8 Tigers** Mr Tig the Tiger
Explore word order by predicting words from previous text Group a range of words that might fit Reinforce knowledge of the term *sentence*	Use poems as models for own writing Compose poetic sentences	**Unit 9 Myself** 'Who Is It?', 'Everybody says' & 'After a Bath'

Scope and Sequence	RED LEVEL BEGINNING NON-FICTION SKILLS	
	Reading Comprehension	**Phonics & Spelling**
Unit 1 Holidays On the Beach	Read and use captions	Secure ability to rhyme and relate this to spelling patterns Explore rhyming patterns Generate rhyming strings Collect words linked to topic
Unit 2 Birthdays Party Time	Read and use captions	Discriminate and segment phonemes in cvc words Represent three phonemes in writing rhyming sets Collect words of personal interest
Unit 3 Food How to make Ice-lollies	Read and follow simple instructions	Recognise critical features of words – words within words Collect words related to topic
Unit 4 Foxes All about Foxes	Understand that the reader does not need to go from start to finish but selects what is needed Predict what a given book might be about from a brief look at both front and back covers	Investigate, read and spell words ending in ... *ck*, *ng*. Identify separate phonemes within words containing clusters Segment clusters into phonemes for spelling
Unit 5 Beans Growing Beans	Use terms 'fiction' and 'non-fiction', noting some of their differing features, e.g. layout, titles, contents page, use of pictures, labelled diagrams	Discriminate, read and spell words with final consonant clusters Identify separate phonemes within words containing clusters Segment clusters into phonemes for spelling
Unit 6 Toys In the Park & Toys	Use simple dictionaries Understand their alphabetical ordering	Secure identification, spelling and reading of initial letter sounds in simple words Discriminate, read and spell words with final consonant clusters Secure alphabetical ordering
Unit 7 Homes Inside a House	Use text to find answers Locate parts of text that give particular information including labelled diagrams and charts	Learn common spelling patterns for the long vowel phonemes ... *ai*, *ie*, *oa* Identify phonemes in speech and writing Use the terms 'vowel' and 'consonant'
Unit 8 Tigers Tigers	Recognise that non-fiction books on similar themes can give different information and present similar information in different ways	Learn common spelling patterns for the long vowel phonemes ... *ee*, *oo*. Segment words into phonemes for spelling Use the terms 'vowel' and 'consonant'
Unit 9 Myself My Body & Growing up	Identify simple questions and use text to find answers Locate parts of text that give particular information including labelled diagrams and charts	Investigate and learn spelling of verbs with 'ed' and 'ing' endings

Grammar & Punctuation	Writing Composition	
Recognise whether captions make sense Recognise full stops and capital letters Understand that a line of writing is not the same as a sentence	Write captions for their own work	**Unit 1 Holidays** On the Beach
Recognise correctly full stops and capital letters Begin using the term *sentence* Begin using full stops to demarcate sentences	Write captions for their own work	**Unit 2 Birthdays** Party Time
Name full stops and capital letters Begin using full stops to demarcate sentences Begin using a capital letter for the personal pronoun 'I'	Write and draw simple instructions and labels	**Unit 3 Food** How to make Ice-lollies
Predict words from preceding words in sentences Investigate words that 'fit' Suggest appropriate alternatives	Assemble information from own experience Use simple sentences to describe, based on reading Write simple non-chronological reports and organise into lists, separate pages, charts	**Unit 4 Foxes** All about Foxes
Continue demarcating sentences in writing with a full stop and a capital letter Use the term *sentence* appropriately	Write labels for drawings and diagrams Produce extended captions	**Unit 5 Beans** Growing Beans
Continue demarcating sentences in writing with a full stop and a capital letter Use the term *sentence* appropriately Use capital letters for names and the start of a sentence	Make own simple dictionary pages Use simple sentences to describe, based on examples from reading Organise in lists	**Unit 6 Toys** In the Park & Toys
Explore word order by re-ordering sentences and discussing reasons why Predict words from previous text Explore words that might 'fit' Reinforce knowledge of the term *sentence*	Use the language and features of non-fiction texts, e.g. labelled diagrams, captions for pictures, to make class books	**Unit 7 Homes** Inside a House
Explore word order by re-ordering sentences and discussing reasons why Reinforce knowledge of the term *sentence*	Write own questions prior to reading for information and record answers	**Unit 8 Tigers** Tigers
Learn common uses of capitalisation, e.g. personal titles, headings, emphasis Add question marks to questions	Use the language and features of non-fiction texts, e.g. labelled diagrams, captions for pictures, to make class books	**Unit 9 Myself** My Body & Growing up

Holidays unit 1

Little Bean

Fiction

National Literacy Strategy

Year 1 Term 1

Range

Fiction: stories with familiar settings

Pupils should be taught:

Text level work

Reading comprehension

4 to read familiar, simple stories and poems independently, to point while reading and make correspondence between words said and read;

5 to describe story settings and incidents and relate them to own experience and that of others;

Word level work

Phonological awareness, phonics and spelling

2 from YR, to practise and secure alphabetic letter knowledge . . .;

3 from YR, to practise and secure the ability to hear initial and final phonemes in CVC words . . .;

4 to discriminate and segment all three phonemes in CVC words;

Word recognition, graphic knowledge and spelling

9 to read on sight . . . high frequency words identified for Year 1 . . . from Appendix List 1;

Sentence level work

Grammatical awareness

4 to write captions and simple sentences, and to re-read, recognising whether or not they make sense, e.g. missing words, wrong word order;

Text level work

Writing composition

9 to write about events in personal experience linked to a variety of familiar incidents from stories;

11 to make simple picture storybooks with sentences, modelling them on basic text conventions, e.g. cover, author's name, title, layout.

Teaching Notes

Poster: Shared reading

Text level work

Explain to the children that the text on the poster is the beginning of a story called *Little Bean's Holiday*, by John Wallace. Ensure that they understand that *Little Bean's Holiday* is the title of the book and John Wallace is the name of the author. If necessary, explain that *author* means the name of the person who wrote the book. Ask the children in which part of a book they would find the book's title and the name of the author (cover, title page).

Read the extract to the children, pointing to the words as you read, and asking them to follow carefully.

Base a class discussion on the following points to establish literal comprehension.

- What are Little Bean and her mum getting ready for?
- What does Little Bean's mum want her to do?
- What is Little Bean told to gather together?

Base a class discussion on the following points to investigate familiar settings and experiences.

- Where do you think this story takes place?
- Have you ever packed for a holiday?
- What sort of things did/would you take with you?
- Could you fit everything you wanted to take in your suitcase?
- What is the most unusual thing you have ever taken on holiday?

Encourage the children to predict what Little Bean might want to take with her. Using the children's suggestions, compile a list of items on the board.

Word level work

Write the letters of the alphabet on the board. Ask the children to pretend that they are going on holiday. For each letter of the alphabet in turn, invite volunteers to suggest something they might take on holiday with them that begins with that letter. Write the item next to the appropriate letter, reading the word aloud several times as you do so, placing emphasis on the initial letter.

Once all (or most) of the letters have an associated object, ask volunteers to suggest other things they might take on holiday, and to indicate where on the list each should be written, depending on its initial letter.

Sentence level work

Select and write on the board a simple sentence from the poster, e.g. *Get together all the things you are taking with you.* Invite a volunteer to read the sentence aloud, then read the sentence as a group. Cover or rub out the word *taking*. Ask another child to read the sentence. Notice that it no longer makes sense. Repeat, deleting a different word each time, and note that, whilst some words can be omitted and the sentence still makes sense (e.g. *all*), others are essential.

Undertake a similar exercise using the same sentence but, this time, jumbling some of the words. Discuss how important it is for words to be in the correct order to make sense.

Pupil's book

Text level work

Introduction

The text in the pupil's book continues the story of *Little Bean's Holiday* and can be used as a whole-class/group text to investigate familiar settings and experiences.

Read through the extract with the children and encourage them to point at the words as you read them.

Discuss:

- what Little Bean wants to pack: Can the children remember what she packs without looking back at the text? Do they think she needs all those things? What do they think she could leave behind?
- what her mum says: Do they think Mum is fair or not? Why?
- how Little Bean reacts: Do they think Little Bean is being silly? What would they have done? Would they rather go away on holiday or have a holiday in the shed?

Reading comprehension

Comprehension Copymaster 1 Fiction is a picture and word matching activity. The children can work in pairs. Encourage the children to say the name of each item and sound the initial letter/blend, then look for the corresponding letter/blend in the list of words. They can draw a line to join each picture to the correct word. More able children could be asked to copy the correct word beside each picture instead.

Children who finish the activity quickly could be asked to use the back of the copymaster to draw and label some of the things they would take on holiday.

Word level work

Letter sounds and the alphabet

Remind the children of the difference between letter sounds and letter names. At this point, assume that letter sounds are the 'short' sounds found in most CVC words (e.g. 'a' in *cat*). Using letter tiles or cards made for the purpose, ask the children to select the five vowel letters ('a', 'e', 'i', 'o', 'u') from the alphabet. Display one of the vowels (e.g. 'a'), then place in front of it any consonant letter (e.g. 'm' + 'a'). Sound out the two letters. Now, by choosing a third letter to add at the end of the word, ask the children to try to make a 'real' word (e.g. 'm' + 'a' + 't'). Repeat until a CVC word has been made using each of the five vowel letters.

This activity can be adapted for whole-class, group or individual work. It can also be varied by choosing a vowel, then adding the *final* consonant to make the 'rime' part of a CVC word before inviting children to add an initial letter to complete the word. It may be necessary to steer them towards frequently used final letters such as 'd', 'g', 'm', 'n', 'p', 't'.

Copy five of the CVC words you have made and, next to each, write a rhyming word. Ask the children to suggest others.

Use **Word Copymaster 1 Fiction** for support with alphabetic letter knowledge and initial phoneme work with CVC words.

The high-frequency words for this unit, to be taught as 'sight recognition' words, are as follows.

red
bed
an
ran
man

Sentence level work

Word order

Having read with the children the passage in the pupil's book, make up some simple, oral sentences about Little Bean, but mix the order of the words, e.g. *Little Bean dog has a*. Write the jumbled sentence on the board, and invite the children to help you to correct it.

Repeat the activity, this time inviting the children to correct the sentence themselves. In each case, use the opportunity to remind the children that sentences need to begin with a capital letter and end with a full stop.

Text level work

Writing composition

Writing Copymaster 1 Fiction provides the opportunity for children to complete sentences based on the story of Little Bean, and to add a picture and sentence of their own, based on what they have read.

As an extension activity, the children could use a folded sheet of A4 paper to make a little book of their own, with one of the following titles:

Little Bean's Toys
Little Bean's Friends
My holiday.

Copymaster answers

Comprehension Copymaster 1

Pupils join each picture with the correct word.

Word Skills Copymaster 1

A *Pupils complete the alphabets.*

B 1 rug
2 sun
3 net
4 hat
5 hut
6 bat
7 cup
8 pan
9 rat

Writing Copymaster 1

A 1 She wants to take her teddy.
2 She wants to take her ball.
3 She wants to take her brush.

B *Individual answers.*

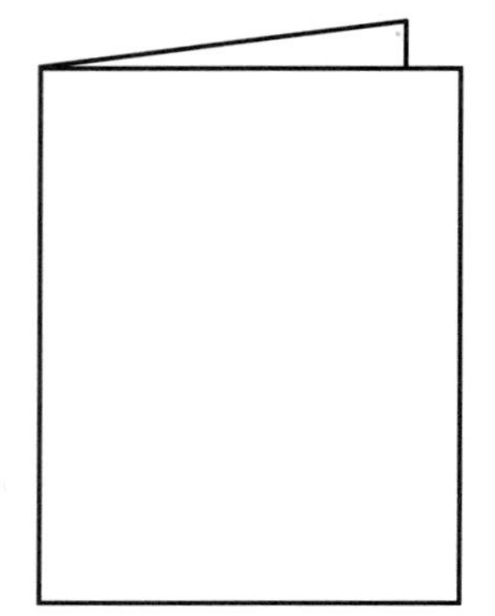

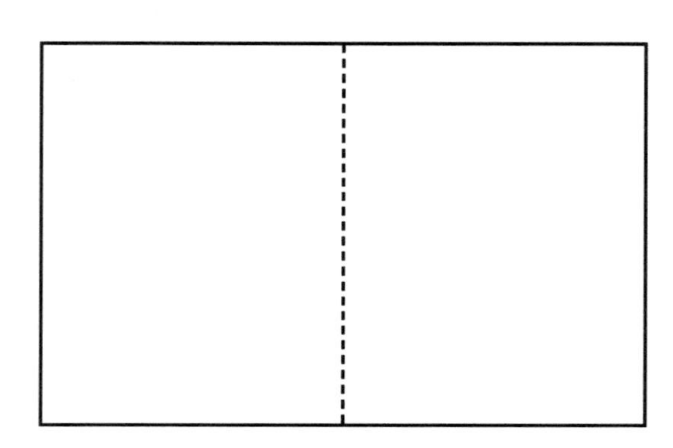

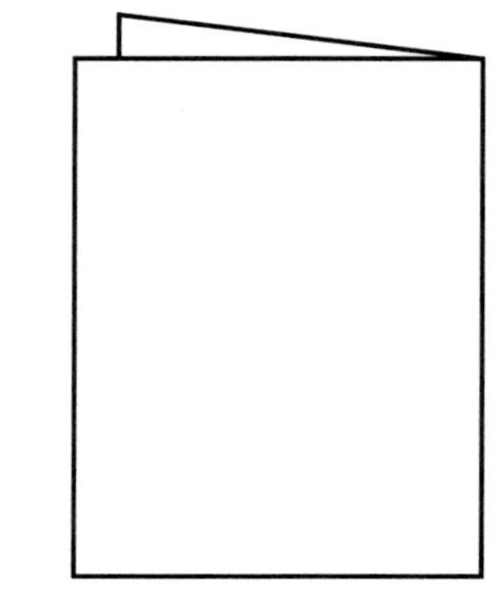

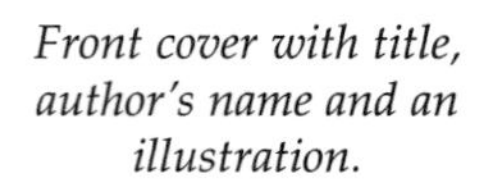

Front cover with title, author's name and an illustration.

There are two inside pages and the back cover acts as a third page; each page has a drawing and a simple sentence.

Little Bean

Little Bean, stop messing around and get ready. We're going on holiday!

Get together all the things you are taking with you.

What things shall I take?

Well, everything you need, Little Bean.

Everything I need. Well, I need ...

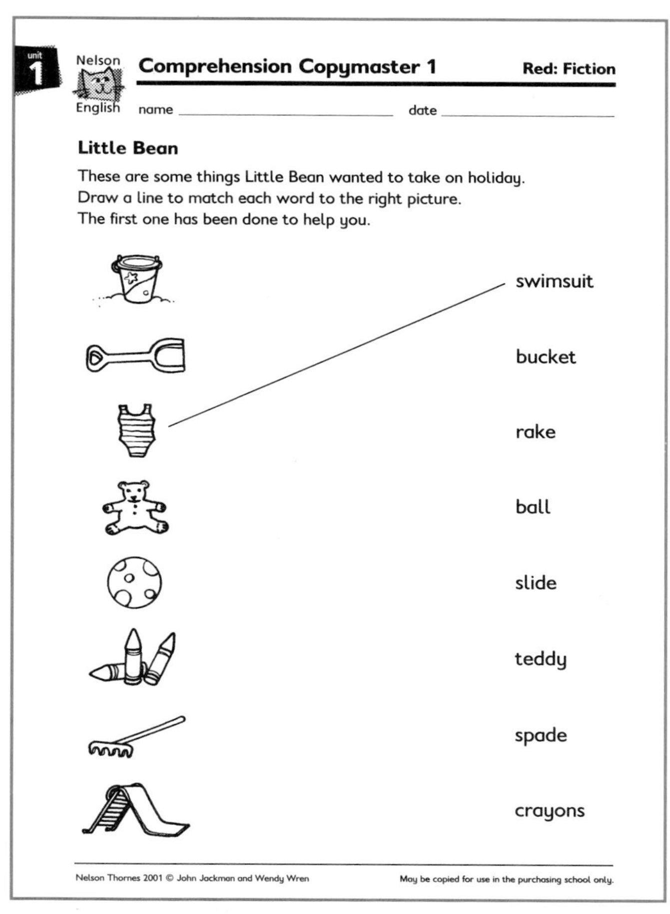

unit 1 Nelson English **Comprehension Copymaster 1** **Red: Fiction**

name ______________ date ______________

Little Bean

These are some things Little Bean wanted to take on holiday.
Draw a line to match each word to the right picture.
The first one has been done to help you.

swimsuit

bucket

rake

ball

slide

teddy

spade

crayons

Nelson Thornes 2001 © John Jackman and Wendy Wren — May be copied for use in the purchasing school only.

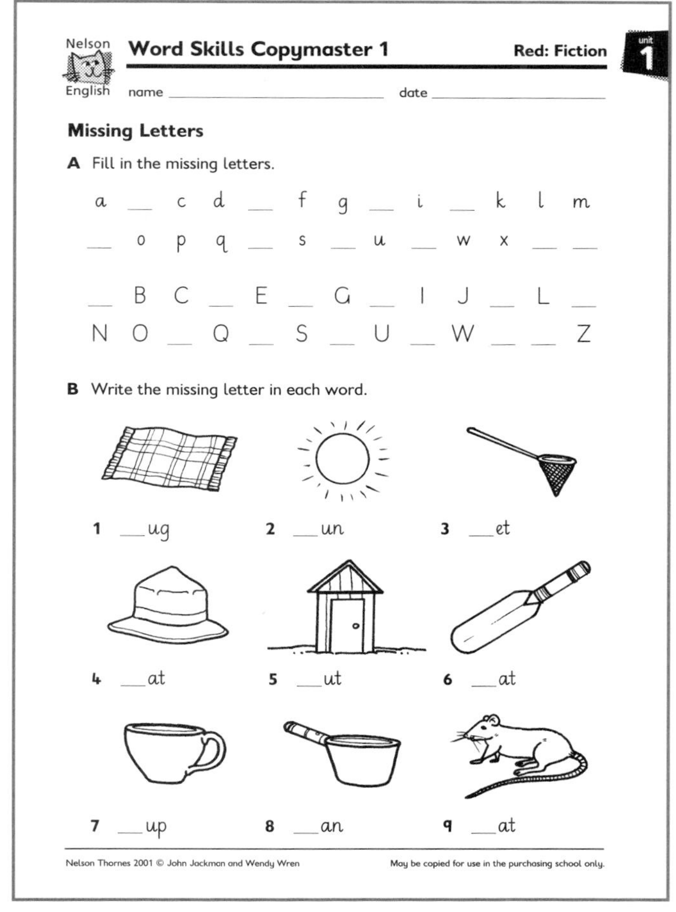

Nelson English **Word Skills Copymaster 1** **Red: Fiction** unit 1

name ______________ date ______________

Missing Letters

A Fill in the missing letters.

a __ c d __ f g __ i __ k l m

__ o p q __ s __ u __ w x __ __

__ B C __ E __ G __ I J __ L __

N O __ Q __ S __ U __ W __ __ Z

B Write the missing letter in each word.

1 __ug 2 __un 3 __et

4 __at 5 __ut 6 __at

7 __up 8 __an 9 __at

Nelson Thornes 2001 © John Jackman and Wendy Wren — May be copied for use in the purchasing school only.

unit 1 Nelson English **Writing Copymaster 1** **Red: Fiction**

name ______________ date ______________

Missing Words

A Complete the sentences.

Little Bean is going on holiday.

1 She wants to take her ______________.

2 She wants to take her ______________.

3 She wants to take her ______________.

B Draw something else Little Bean wants to take on holiday.
Write a sentence about your picture.

____

____

____

____

Holidays unit 1

On the Beach

Non-fiction

National Literacy Strategy

Year 1 Term 1

Range

Non-fiction: signs, labels, captions . . .

Pupils should be taught:

Text level work

Reading comprehension

12 to read and use captions, e.g. labels around the school, on equipment;

Word level work

Phonological awareness, phonics and spelling

1 from YR, to practise and secure the ability to rhyme, and to relate this to spelling patterns through:
- exploring and playing with rhyming patterns;
- generating rhyming strings, e.g. *fat*, *hat*, *pat*;

Word recognition, graphic knowledge and spelling

9 to read on sight . . . high frequency words identified for Year 1 . . . from Appendix List 1;

Vocabulary extension

12 new words from reading and shared experiences, and to make collections of personal interest or significant words and words linked to particular topics;

Sentence level work

Grammatical awareness

4 to write captions and simple sentences, and to re-read, recognising whether or not they make sense, e.g. missing words, wrong word order;

Sentence construction and punctuation

5 to recognise full stops and capital letters when reading, and name them correctly;

6 to begin using the term *sentence* to identify sentences in text;

7 that a line of writing is not necessarily the same as a sentence;

8 to begin using full stops to demarcate sentences;

Text level work

Writing composition

14 to write captions for their own work, e.g. for display, in class books.

Teaching Notes

Poster: Shared reading

Text level work

Display the poster and ask the children what they can see. Encourage them to describe what they see in detail. For example, if a child says, 'I can see a bucket'. Ask, 'What colour is it?', 'Where is it?', etc. Point out the words on the vocabulary strip as the children identify the objects in the picture, or ask individuals to point them out.

Encourage the children to talk about their own experiences on the beach, prompting them with questions such as:

- Have you ever been to the beach?
- What did you do there?
- Do you like the beach?
- Did you paddle in the sea?

Discuss the text that appears within the beach scene on the poster, such as shop names, signposts, etc. Encourage the children to recall where they have seen similar signs around the school/local area.

Remind the children of the text in the parallel Fiction unit (Little Bean). Ask individuals to come forward and ring words in the vocabulary strip on the poster which are the names of items people take to the beach, e.g. *buckets*, *spades*, etc. Others can be asked to identify words that are the names of objects found naturally on the beach, e.g. *crab*, *shells*, etc.

The poster should be left on display while the children are working on this unit.

Word level work

Read together the vocabulary strip on the poster, then select a word that offers straightforward rhyming opportunities with CVC or other short words, e.g. *sand*, and invite the children to suggest words that rhyme, e.g. *and, band, hand, land*. Write up the words on the board as they are suggested, so children can see the spelling patterns. Repeat with other words from the poster, such as *sun* (*bun, fun, gun, run*), *fish* (*dish, wish*) and *shell* (*bell, fell, sell, tell, well*), etc.

This is a good opportunity to encourage some children to start a personal spelling dictionary or spelling 'log'. Suggest that they copy an appropriate number of the word lists into their books and possibly add at least one other word of their own, having checked its spelling with an adult.

Use **Word Copymaster 1 Non-fiction** for support. More able children could copy the rhyming pairs on the back of the copymaster or in their spelling log, rather than joining them with lines. They could also be asked to add other rhyming words of their own.

Sentence level work

Having explored the 'environmental text' on the poster (i.e. the signs), and considered how this is intended to give information (e.g. the deckchair sign tells us how much it costs to hire a deckchair), discuss how such text differs from a sentence. Whilst a sign can be used to give information in a particular context, a sentence usually gives more specific information.

Pupil's book

Text level work

Introduction

The stimulus material continues the theme of the beach. There are four pictures of beach scenes, each with a simple caption.

Discuss the pictures and read through the captions with the children. Encourage them to point to each word as you read it.

Discuss which word in each sentence could be used as a label for the picture. For example:
picture 1: waves
picture 2: children/sand-castle
picture 3: ice-cream
picture 4: sun.

Reading comprehension

Comprehension Copymaster 1 Non-fiction is a picture and word matching activity. The children can work in pairs. Encourage the children to say the name of each item and sound the initial letter/blend, then look for the corresponding letter/blend in the list of words. They can draw a line to join each picture to the correct word. More able children could be asked to copy the correct word beside each picture instead.

Children who finish the activity quickly could be asked to use the back of the copymaster to draw and label some other things they might see on the beach.

Word level work

CVC rhyming words

Begin by repeating the activity carried out in the parallel Fiction unit, using letter tiles or cards to create CVC words, starting with the vowel (see page 23). This time, after each word has been formed, remove the initial letter and try to find other consonants that might be added to form other (rhyming) words, e.g. *bat* (*cat, fat, hat, mat, sat, rat*). For a useful reference list of other similar letter patterns and word groups, see the Nelson Spelling *Teacher's Book*.

The high-frequency words for this unit, to be taught as 'sight recognition' words, are as follows.

so
by
had
has
us

Sentence level work

Capital letters and full stops

Copy one of the sentences from the book on to the board, but omit the capital letter and the full stop. Ask the children to spot the deliberate mistake by checking what you have written against the sentence in the pupil's book. Next, invite a volunteer to make up a sentence about the poster picture. Write the sentence on the board, again omitting the capital letter and the full stop. Ask the child who offered the sentence, or another child if appropriate, to identify the mistake and come forward to correct the sentence.

Through discussion, help the children to discover why capital letters at the beginning of sentences and full stops at the end are important. To do this, write two or three simple sentences on the board as continuous text, and explore how difficult it is to read sensibly without punctuation.

Text level work

Writing composition

Writing Copymaster 1 Non-fiction gives children the opportunity to complete captions for two of the pictures from the pupil's book.

They are then asked to draw their own beach picture and to write a simple caption for it.

Copymaster answers

Comprehension Copymaster 1

Pupils join each picture with the correct word.

Word Skills Copymaster 1

A 1 jug
2 pen
3 mug
4 pin
5 man
6 bin
7 log
8 van
9 dog
10 map
11 hen
12 cap

B *Pupils should draw lines to connect the following pairs:*

ug	mug
pen	hen
pin	bin
man	van
log	dog
map	cap

Writing Copymaster 1

A 1 The <u>waves</u> are big.
2 It is hot in the <u>sun</u>.

B *Individual answers.*

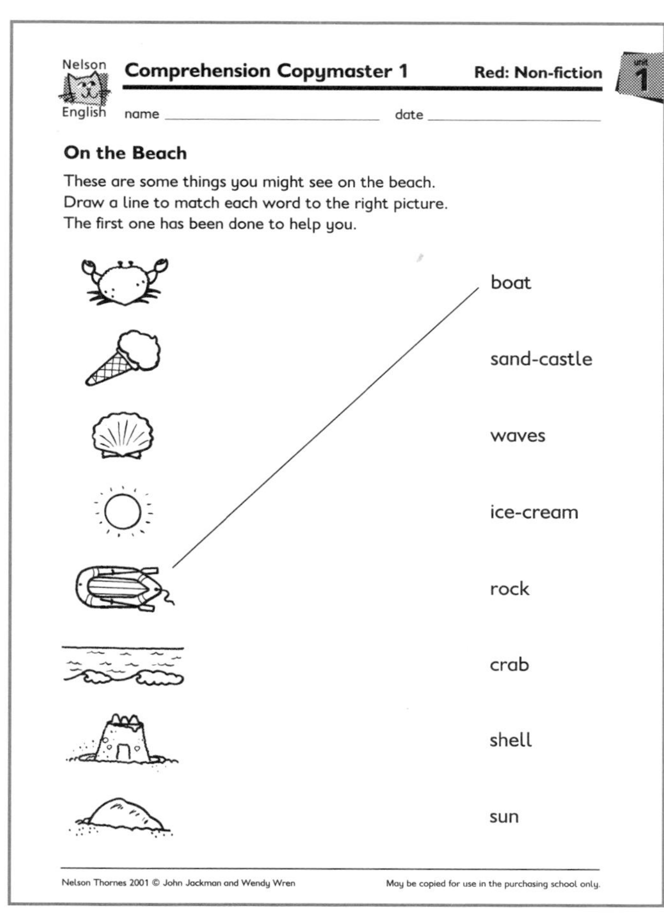

Nelson English

Comprehension Copymaster 1 — Red: Non-fiction

name ____________ date ____________

On the Beach

These are some things you might see on the beach.
Draw a line to match each word to the right picture.
The first one has been done to help you.

boat

sand-castle

waves

ice-cream

rock

crab

shell

sun

Nelson Thornes 2001 © John Jackman and Wendy Wren — May be copied for use in the purchasing school only.

Nelson English

Word Skills Copymaster 1 — Red: Non-fiction

name ____________ date ____________

Rhyming Words

A Fill in the missing letters.
They are all vowels: **a e i o u**

1 j__g
2 p__n
3 m__g
4 p__n
5 m__n
6 b__n
7 l__g
8 v__n
9 d__g
10 m__p
11 h__n
12 c__p

B Draw lines to join the pairs of words that rhyme.

Nelson Thornes 2001 © John Jackman and Wendy Wren — May be copied for use in the purchasing school only.

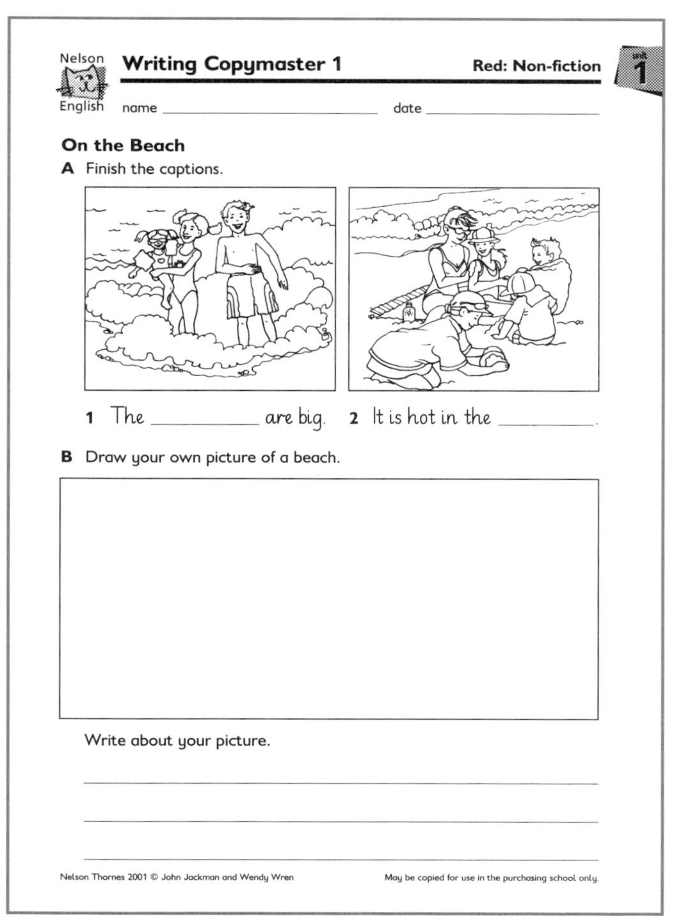

Nelson English

Writing Copymaster 1 — Red: Non-fiction

name ____________ date ____________

On the Beach

A Finish the captions.

1 The ________ are big.
2 It is hot in the ________.

B Draw your own picture of a beach.

Write about your picture.

Nelson Thornes 2001 © John Jackman and Wendy Wren — May be copied for use in the purchasing school only.

Duncan's Tree House

Fiction

National Literacy Strategy

Year 1 Term 1

Range

Fiction: stories with familiar settings

Pupils should be taught:

Text level work

Reading comprehension

5 to describe story settings and incidents and relate them to own experience and that of others;

Word level work

Phonological awareness, phonics and spelling

4 to discriminate and segment all three phonemes in CVC words;

6 to represent in writing the three phonemes in CVC words, spelling them first in rhyming sets, then in non-rhyming sets;

Word recognition, graphic knowledge and spelling

9 to read on sight . . . high frequency words identified for Year 1 . . . from Appendix List 1;

Sentence level work

Sentence construction and punctuation

5 to recognise full stops and capital letters when reading, and name them correctly;

6 to begin using the term sentence to identify sentences in text;

7 that a line of writing is not necessarily the same as a sentence;

8 to begin using full stops to demarcate sentences;

Text level work

Writing composition

9 to write about events in personal experience linked to a variety of familiar incidents from stories.

Teaching Notes

Poster: Shared reading

Text level work

The same text appears on the poster and in the pupil's book so the following discussion work can be done using either.

Explain to the children that the text passage is the beginning of a story called *Duncan's Tree House* by Amanda Vesey. Ensure they understand that *Duncan's Tree House* is the title of the book and Amanda Vesey is the name of the author. If necessary, recap on the definition of *author*. Ask the children in which part of a book they would find the book's title and the name of the author (cover, title page).

Read the extract to the children, pointing to the words as you read, and asking them to follow carefully.

Base a class discussion on the following questions to establish literal comprehension.

- What did Duncan's father do for a living?
- What was Duncan given for his birthday?
- Where had Duncan's father made the tree house?
- Where did he fix it?
- What did Duncan say to his parents when he saw the tree house?
- What did Duncan make for the tree house?

Base a class discussion on the following points to investigate familiar settings and experiences.

- What does the outside of the tree house look like? (based on pictures)
- What is the inside of the tree house like? (based on pictures and text)
- Allow the discussion to broaden into the children's own experiences of:
  - tree houses, dens or camps – encourage the children to describe these in detail

- birthday presents, presents they have received/would like to receive, presents they have given
- If they had Duncan's tree house, what would they like to have inside?
- What would they use the tree house for?
- Who would be allowed in?
- Why do they think Duncan wanted a sign for his tree house?
- Would they have a sign?
- If so, what would it say?

Word level work

Select some simple CVC words from the poster (e.g. *him, had, bed, rug, tin*) and write them on the board. Sound the letters clearly as you write them, inviting the children to join in with you. Next, write the letters randomly over the board and point to each in turn, asking the children to sound them. Return to the words, and ask volunteers to sound out the letters of each word before saying the word.

For each CVC word chosen from the poster, ask volunteers to suggest other CVC words that rhyme with it, e.g. *him* (*Kim, Tim*); *had* (*bad, dad, fad, lad, mad, pad, sad*); *bed* (*fed, led, Ned, red, Ted, wed*); *rug* (*bug, dug, hug, jug, lug, mug, tug*); *tin* (*bin, din, fin, pin, sin, win*). Pupils may suggest non-CVC words, such as *said* or *head* to rhyme with *bed*, so this activity provides a good opportunity to begin to alert children to the vagaries of English, in which certain phonemes can be represented by more than one grapheme. For example, short 'e' (as in *bed*) is also represented by 'ai' (as in *said*) and 'ea' (as in *dead*).

Word Skills Copymaster 2 Fiction provides practice in forming CVC words. Pupils add the second and third letters of each word. More able pupils could be asked to add one or more other words that rhyme with each word on the copymaster.

Sentence level work

Having shared the text on the poster, ask a volunteer to point to the first capital letter. Ask why this first letter (*O*) should be a capital. Next ask how we know where this first sentence ends (i.e. full stop). Explain that capital letters are not only used at the beginning of a sentence, but are also used at the beginning of a person's name (e.g. *Duncan*).

Together, identify other sentences on the poster. Draw out the observation that a line of text is not always a 'proper' sentence, and that sentences are sometimes less than a line in length and often more than a line. Ask a volunteer to point out examples of each on the poster.

Pupil's book

Text level work

Introduction

The text passage is the same as that on the poster, which will allow groups or individuals to work on the text at the same time. In group/class discussion look at the pictures and ask the children to describe the inside and outside of the tree house in detail, e.g. blanket (checked/tartan/red), rug (brightly coloured/striped), etc., in preparation for the descriptive writing work on the Writing copymaster. Prompt the children to think of size, shape, colour, texture, pattern, etc.

Reading comprehension

Comprehension Copymaster 2 Fiction requires children to answer simple questions about the story. The questions can be approached as a class discussion, in guided or independently working groups, or individually.

Word level work

CVC rhyming words

Depending on how well the children have grasped the work undertaken with the poster, either ask them to undertake the work again individually or in small groups, selecting the CVC words themselves, or offer other CVC words for the children to sound and for which to write sets of rhyming words. For a useful reference list of CVC words with similar letter patterns and word groups, see the Nelson Spelling *Teacher's Book*.

The high-frequency words for this unit, to be taught as 'sight recognition' words, are as follows.

do
not
got
her
his

Sentence level work

Capital letters and full stops

Through discussion, help the children to discover why sentences need a capital letter at the beginning and a full stop at the end. Write this jumbled sentence on the board: *tree house was the bed. a Inside* and ask the children how the sentence can be rearranged to make sense. Point out the clues offered by the capital letter and full stop. The children should write the sentence correctly and, if appropriate, could be asked to add another short sentence of their own about the tree house.

Text level work

Writing composition

To write about events from personal experience and link them to events in stories may prove to be quite an ambitious task for some children. Those whom you judge to be capable can write on their own, describing either:

- their own tree house, den, camp or favourite place (either real or imagined)
- the best birthday present they have received or would like to receive.

Encourage the children to work in draft and to discuss with you what they have written before copying it neatly and, if time allows, illustrating it.

For those children who are not yet able to write independently, **Writing Copymaster 2 Fiction** will provide support.

Copymaster answers

Comprehension Copymaster 2

1 No
2 Yes
3 No
4 Yes
5 No
6 Yes
7 No
8 Yes

Word Skills Copymaster 2

Children should complete the following labels:
mop, jug, mat, pen, bed, bin, box, pan, mug, dog

Writing Copymaster 2

Individual answers.

Duncan's Tree House

On his birthday, Duncan's parents gave him a tree house.

Duncan's father was a builder. He had made the tree house in his workshop and he had fixed it to the tree the night before Duncan's birthday, when Duncan was asleep.

It was a complete surprise to Duncan.

Inside the tree house was a camp bed and a rug and a table and a chair and a shelf with cups and plates on it. There was a bookcase and a tin box for keeping things in. The window had real glass in it, and opened and shut.

Duncan leaned out of the window and waved to his parents in the garden below.

"Thank you!" yelled Duncan. "I'll put up a sign so that everyone will know whose house it is."

He carved DUNCAN'S TREE HOUSE with his penknife on a piece of wood, and painted it.

Then he nailed it to the hand rail outside his front door.

Nelson English — Red Level: Fiction — unit 2

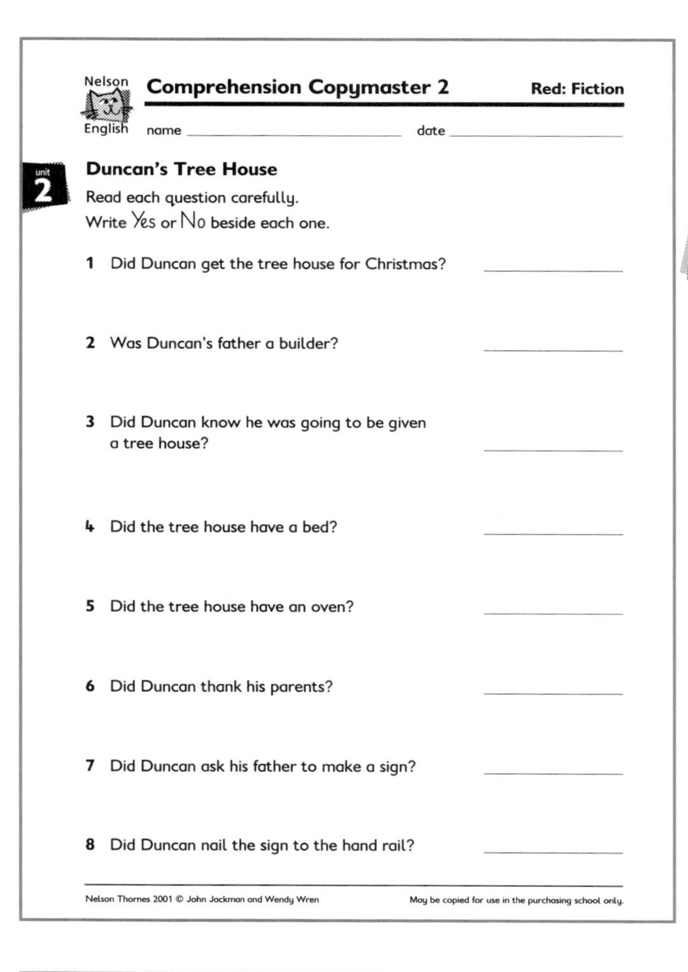

Nelson English

Comprehension Copymaster 2 — Red: Fiction

name ______________ date ______________

unit 2

Duncan's Tree House

Read each question carefully.
Write Yes or No beside each one.

1 Did Duncan get the tree house for Christmas? ______

2 Was Duncan's father a builder? ______

3 Did Duncan know he was going to be given a tree house? ______

4 Did the tree house have a bed? ______

5 Did the tree house have an oven? ______

6 Did Duncan thank his parents? ______

7 Did Duncan ask his father to make a sign? ______

8 Did Duncan nail the sign to the hand rail? ______

unit 2

Nelson English

Word Skills Copymaster 2 — Red: Fiction

name ______________ date ______________

unit 2

Labels

Finish the labels.

Nelson English

Writing Copymaster 2 — Red: Fiction

name ______________ date ______________

unit 2

My Birthday

A Finish the sentences.

1 I am ______________ years old.

2 My birthday is on ______________.

3 The birthday present I would like best is ______________ because ______________ ______________.

B Draw the present you would like. Write some words to describe the present.

____
____
____
____
____
____
____
____

Birthdays unit 2

Party Time

Non-fiction

National Literacy Strategy

Year 1 Term 1

Range

Non-fiction: signs, labels, captions . . .

Pupils should be taught:

Text level work

Reading comprehension

12 to read and use captions, e.g. labels around the school, on equipment;

Word level work

Phonological awareness, phonics and spelling

4 to discriminate and segment all three phonemes in CVC words;

6 to represent in writing the three phonemes in CVC words, spelling them first in rhyming sets, then in non-rhyming sets;

Word recognition, graphic knowledge and spelling

9 to read on sight . . . high frequency words identified for Year 1 . . . from Appendix List 1;

Vocabulary extension

12 new words from reading and shared experiences, and to make collections of personal interest or significant words and words linked to particular topics;

Sentence level work

Sentence construction and punctuation

5 to recognise full stops and capital letters when reading, and name them correctly;

6 to begin using the term *sentence* to identify sentences in text;

7 that a line of writing is not necessarily the same as a sentence;

8 to begin using full stops to demarcate sentences;

Text level work

Writing composition

14 to write captions for their own work, e.g. for display, in class books.

Teaching Notes

Poster: Shared reading

Text level work

Display the poster and ask the children what they can see. Encourage them to describe what they see in detail, concentrating on the actions of the children on the poster.

Point out the words on the vocabulary strip as the children identify the various activities, or ask individuals to point them out.

Ask the children to explain how the two games on the poster (musical chairs and pin the tail on the donkey) are played, how you can be 'out' and how you can win.

Encourage the children to relate their own diverse experiences of birthdays, birthday parties and treats.

Word level work

Some of the CVC words used in this unit are also to be found in the parallel Fiction unit (Duncan's Tree House). This is to consolidate the previous learning, and to help the children begin to transfer the skills learnt to other similarly structured words.

Select some simple CVC words illustrated on the poster and write them on the board (e.g. *fun*, *sit*, *cat*, *pop*). Sound the letters clearly as you write them, inviting the children to join with you. Next, write the letters randomly over the board and point to each in turn, asking the children to sound them. Return to the words and ask volunteers to sound out the letters of each word before saying the word.

Read the words one by one, asking volunteers to suggest other CVC words to rhyme with each, e.g. *fun* (*bun, gun, run, sun*); *sit* (*bit, fit, hit, lit, pit, wit*); *win* (*bin, din, fin, pin, sin, tin*); *cat* (*bat, fat, hat, sat, mat, rat*); *pin* (*bin, din, fin, sin, tin, win*); *pop* (*top, hop, lop, mop*). If possible, encourage volunteers to act as scribes to write the words in rhyming lists on the board.

If they haven't previously done so, now would be a suitable time for some children to start compiling personal spelling dictionaries, or spelling 'logs'. Suggest that they copy an appropriate number of the 'party' words into their books and possibly add at least one other word of their own, having checked its spelling with an adult.

Sentence level work

Read the vocabulary strip together. Then invite the children to discuss a party that they recall, and to offer a sentence about that party, using one of the words in the vocabulary strip. Write their sentences on the board, omitting the initial capital letter and full stop in each sentence. Ask selected children to come forward to point out and/or correct the mistakes.

Pupil's book

Text level work

Introduction

The stimulus material continues the theme of parties, showing a birthday tea party in full swing. Objects in the picture are labelled.

Discuss the picture with the children, encouraging them to describe in detail what they see.

Ask for suggestions for a caption. Obviously, 'The birthday party' will be suggested but encourage the children to look more closely at what is happening and come up with something more original.

Reading comprehension

Comprehension Copymaster 2 Non-fiction requires the children to 'read' the picture for literal information to complete the sentences. The comprehension questions can be approached as a class discussion, in guided or independently working groups, or individually.

Word level work

CVC rhyming words

Discuss the picture of the party and, from it, help the children to write the following words: *bun, hat, dog*. Now invite the children to select one or more of the words and to make as many other words as possible by changing just one letter of the selected words, e.g. *bun* (*fun, run, sun, Ben, ban, bin, but, bug, bus*, etc.).

Use **Word Skills Copymaster 2 Non-fiction** for further practice with CVC words, if required. In part A, children are asked to select from three similar CVC words the correct one to go with each picture. In part B, they identify rhyming words, which provides practice in identifying common letter patterns.

The high-frequency words for this unit, to be taught as 'sight recognition' words, are as follows.

into
some
love
call
ball

Sentence level work

Capital letters and full stops

Write *It is fun at the party*. Ask the children to read the sentence with you, then write *red balloon* and ask the children which is a 'proper' sentence and how they can tell (i.e. by the capital letter and full stop). They should copy the sentence and, if appropriate, add another short sentence of their own about the party, with a capital letter and a full stop.

Text level work

Writing composition

Children who are able should draw a picture of a birthday celebration which they have attended or from their imagination. They should write a sentence as a caption for the picture.

Children for whom independent writing is too ambitious can complete **Writing Copymaster 2 Non-fiction**, which provides six pictures to colour and caption. They depict objects from the picture in the pupil's book. The children should be encouraged to find the label from the picture in their book, but to write more than *a jug, a hat*, etc. by including a descriptive word such as the colour they have made the object (e.g. *the red jug*), the size of the object (e.g. *the big hat*), etc.

Copymaster answers

unit 2

Comprehension Copymaster 2

1 The dog is under the table.
2 The cake looks like a car.
3 The children are wearing hats.
4 The boy spills his drink.
5 The food is on the table.

Word Copymaster 2

A 1 hat
2 hug
3 hit
4 hop

B 1 jam, ham, ram
2 men, ten, hen
3 fun, bun, run

Writing Copymaster 2

Individual answers.

Nelson English **Comprehension Copymaster 2** Red: Non-fiction

name ______________ date ______________

Missing Words

Look at the picture on pages 6 and 7 of your book.
Use the words in the box to finish the sentences.

table	drink	car	children	dog

1 The ______________ is under the table.

2 The cake looks like a ______________.

3 The ______________ are wearing hats.

4 The boy spills his ______________.

5 The food is on the ______________.

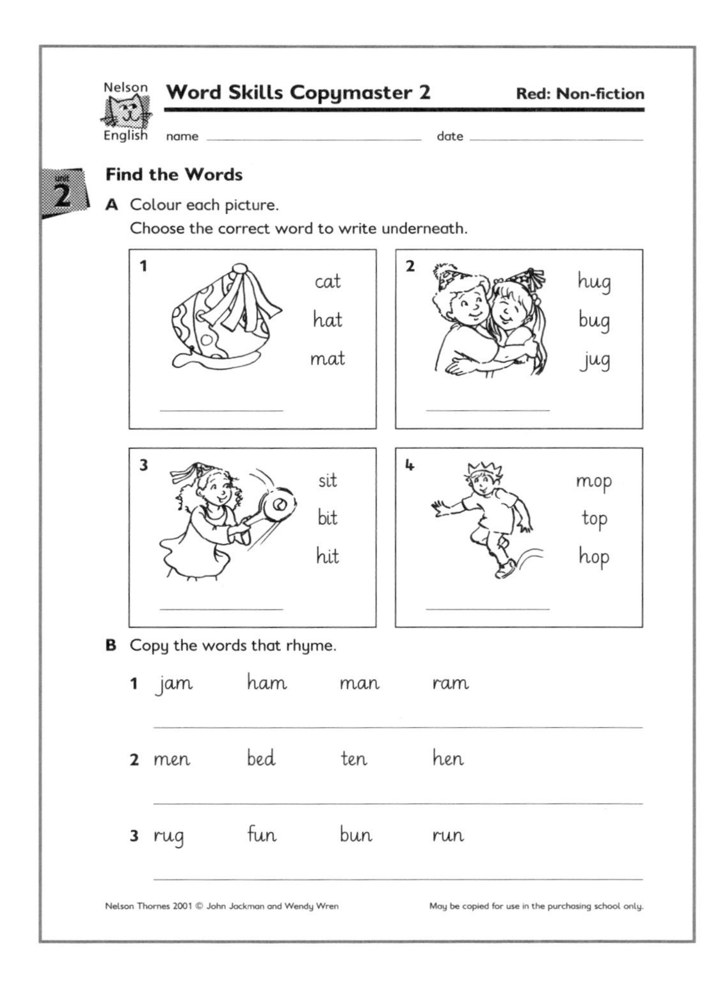

Nelson English **Word Skills Copymaster 2** Red: Non-fiction

name ______________ date ______________

Find the Words

A Colour each picture.
Choose the correct word to write underneath.

1 cat hat mat

2 hug bug jug

3 sit bit hit

4 mop top hop

B Copy the words that rhyme.

1 jam ham man ram

2 men bed ten hen

3 rug fun bun run

Nelson English **Writing Copymaster 2** Red: Non-fiction

name ______________ date ______________

At the Party

Colour the pictures.
Write a caption for each picture.

1 2 3 4 5 6

unit 2

'Jelly on the Plate' & 'The Pancake'

Fiction

National Literacy Strategy

Year 1 Term 1

Range

Fiction: rhymes with predictable and repetitive patterns

Pupils should be taught:

Text level work

Reading comprehension

6 to recite stories and rhymes with predictable and repeating patterns, extemporising on patterns orally by substituting words and phrases, extending patterns, inventing patterns and playing with rhyme;

Word level work

Word recognition, graphic knowledge and spelling

9 to read on sight . . . high frequency words identified for Year 1 . . . from Appendix List 1;

10 to recognise the critical features of words, e.g. length, common spelling patterns and words within words;

Sentence level work

Sentence construction and punctuation

5 to recognise full stops and capital letters when reading, and name them correctly;

7 that a line of writing is not necessarily the same as a sentence;

8 to begin using full stops to demarcate sentences;

Text level work

Writing composition

10 to use rhymes and patterned stories as models for their own writing.

Teaching Notes

Poster: Shared reading

Text level work

Read 'The Pancake' to/with the children. Ask them to identify the title of the poem.

Ask the children to mime the actions of the poem while you read it again. Work towards the children reciting the poem and doing the actions at the same time.

Can they pick out the rhyming words? Can they think of other words that rhyme with *pan* and *can*?

Discuss and list other words which could be used in the poem, which might include the following examples:

Cooking verbs:	Utensil nouns:	Food nouns:
beat	tin	pastry
sift	tray	cake
roll	plate	eggs
heat	pot	soup
boil	bowl	cabbage
chop	dish	buns
cut		sugar
cook		carrots
pour		biscuits
make		pizza
bake		chips
slice		scones

To be strictly true to the rhythm of the poem, the food noun should have two syllables but, because of its structure, the poem will work just as well with a single-syllable food. The two rhyming words, however, must be single syllable.

Either as a class or in groups, the children can experiment with substituting words, for example:

Roll the pastry,
Cut the pastry,
    Pop it in the tray;

Heat the pastry,
Cook the pastry,
    Eat it warm that day.

Mix the soup,
Stir the soup,
    Pop it in the pot;

Warm the soup.
Pour the soup,
    Eat it while it's hot.

Word level work

Use the poster to identify some CVC words, i.e. *mix*, *pop*, *pan*, *can*. Write these across the board. Ask the children what they notice about *pan* and *can*. If no one spots the common rime, write one below the other. Once the children have realised the rhyming possibilities, ask them to suggest other rhyming words both for *pan* and *can* and for the other CVC words. At your discretion, introduce other CVC words, preferably relevant to other current work. Ask the children, in pairs or groups, to find rhyming words.

Following the above activity, write on the board the words *can* and *pan*. This time, ask the children to suggest CVC words that begin with the same first two letters, but have a different final phoneme, e.g. *can: cab, cad, cap, [car], cat; pan: pad, Pam, pat, [paw], [pay].* If the words in brackets are offered, use this opportunity to remind the children that some groups of letters can make different sounds.

Sentence level work

Discuss with the children how poems and rhymes are different from 'ordinary' writing (i.e. prose). Having discussed the rhyming characteristics and the rhythm of the poem, look at the lines of poetry and draw out the useful lesson that, in poems as in other writing, a line is not synonymous with a sentence.

Pupil's book

Text level work

Introduction

As well as appearing on the poster, the poem 'The Pancake' can also be found in the pupil's book, along with 'Jelly on the Plate'. Read both the poems with the children and, if the poster has not been used, go through the teacher's notes and activities for 'The Pancake'.

Most of the children should be familiar with 'Jelly on the Plate'. It is a simple poem they can learn and recite.

Discuss the phrase *wibble, wobble* with the children. What does it tell us about the jelly? (How it moves.) Encourage the children to notice how the words *wibble* and *wobble* sound alike and also sound a bit like the movement they describe. Can they think of other real or 'made up' words that are like this (e.g. *jiggle, joggle; shudder, shiver*)?

Explore four-syllable substitute phrases to describe the jelly, for example:

What it looks like:	red and shiny
What it tastes like:	sweet and fruity
What it feels like:	soft and squashy
	cold and slimy
What it smells like	rich and fruity.

unit 3

Reading comprehension

Comprehension Copymaster 3 Fiction requires children to pick out literal information from the two poems, then select their favourite food, draw and write about it. The written work can vary from a simple descriptive phrase to several sentences, depending on individual ability.

The comprehension questions can be approached as a class discussion, in guided or independently working groups, or individually.

Word level work

Words within words

Introduce the 'hidden words' game. Explain that words often 'hide' in longer words. Write on the board the word *pancake* from the poem. Ask selected children if they can see smaller words within it, i.e. *pan, a, an, cake*. Repeat with *catch* (*cat, a, at*).

Select other words from poems with which the class are familiar and ask them to copy each word and then find as many smaller words as possible within that word.

If children have difficulty finding smaller words within words, it may help to provide letter cards with which to spell out the longer word. The cards can be spaced out or grouped together to help children 'see' the smaller words.

Word Skills Copymaster 3 Fiction provides practice with some of the irregular, but significant, words required in the early stages of independent writing.

The high-frequency words for this unit, to be taught as 'sight recognition' words, are as follows.

him
have
did
dig
off

Sentence level work

Capital letters and full stops

Write on the board the jumbled sentence *is on the plate. big red jelly* and ask the children to write it correctly. Ask them whether they can spot any clues (i.e. the capital letter and the full stop). They should copy the corrected sentence and, if appropriate, add another short sentence of their own about the picture in the book, ensuring they use a capital letter and a full stop. Also, emphasise the fact that sentences are more than collections of words – sentences need to make sense.

Text level work

Writing composition

Following on from the poster/pupil's book discussion, the children should write their own poems using 'The Pancake' and 'Jelly on the Plate' as models. For children who need support, **Writing Copymaster 3 Fiction** provides a framework for the children to fill in to complete the poems.

Copymaster answers

Comprehension Copymaster 3

A 1 jelly pancakes
2 *Two of the following:* mix, stir, fry, toss, catch
3 wibble wobble

B *Individual answers.*

Word Skills Copymaster 3

A *Pupils trace and copy the words.*

B 1 Tom says he likes jelly.
2 His sister says she likes jelly too.
3 My mum gave me a bowl of jelly.
4 "Can we have some jelly?" asked Lucy and Paul.

C *Pupils trace and copy the words.*

D 1 I live ~~near~~ my friend.
2 I will ~~give~~ her some of my pancakes.
3 She says she will ~~give~~ me some of her jelly.

Writing Copymaster 3

Individual answers.

Nelson English

Comprehension Copymaster 3 — Red: Fiction

name ______________________ date ______________________

unit 3

Food Poems

A Look at the poems in your book.

1 What two foods are the poems about?

______________________ ______________________

2 Look at 'The Pancake'. Copy two words that tell you what you can do with a pancake.

______________________ ______________________

3 Look at 'Jelly on the Plate'. Copy the two words that tell you how the jelly moves.

______________________ ______________________

B Draw your favourite food. Write about it.

unit 3

Nelson English

Word Skills Copymaster 3 — Red: Fiction

name ______________________ date ______________________

Tricky Words

A Trace and then copy the words.

1 he he he ________ ________ ________
2 we we we ________ ________ ________
3 me me me ________ ________ ________
4 she she she ________ ________ ________

B Write he or me or we or she in each sentence.

1 Tom says ________ likes jelly.
2 His sister says ________ likes jelly too.
3 My mum gave ________ a bowl of jelly.
4 "Can ________ have some jelly?" asked Lucy and Paul.

C Trace and copy the words.

1 live live live ________ ________ ________
2 give give give ________ ________ ________

D Write live or give in each sentence.

1 I ________ near my friend.
2 I will ________ her some of my pancakes.
3 She says she will ________ me some of her jelly.

unit 3

Nelson English

Writing Copymaster 3 — Red: Fiction

name ______________________ date ______________________

Food Poems

________________ on the Plate

________ on the plate,
________ on the plate,
________ , ________ ,
________ , ________ ,
________ on the plate.

The ________________

________ a ________ ,
________ a ________ ,
Pop it in ________________ ;

________ the ________ ,
________ the ________ ,
________________________ .

unit 3

Food

unit 3

How to make Ice-lollies

Non-fiction

National Literacy Strategy

Year 1 Term 1

Range

Non-fiction: instructions

Pupils should be taught:

Text level work

Reading comprehension

13 to read and follow simple instructions, e.g. for classroom routines, lists for groups in workbooks;

Word level work

Word recognition, graphic knowledge and spelling

9 to read on sight . . . high frequency words identified for Year 1 . . . from Appendix List 1;

10 to recognise the critical features of words, e.g. length, common spelling patterns and words within words;

Vocabulary extension

12 new words from reading and shared experiences, and to make collections of personal interest or significant words and words linked to particular topics;

Sentence level work

Sentence construction and punctuation

5 to recognise full stops and capital letters when reading, and name them correctly;

7 that a line of writing is not necessarily the same as a sentence;

8 to begin using full stops to demarcate sentences;

9 to use a capital letter for the personal pronoun 'I' and for the start of a sentence;

Text level work

Writing composition

16 to write and draw simple instructions and labels for everyday classroom use, e.g. in role play area, for equipment.

Teaching Notes

Poster: Shared reading

Text level work

Display the poster and ask the children what they think is happening in the four pictures. Prompt them with questions such as:

- What do the pictures show you how to do?
- Would it make a difference if the pictures were in a different order?

Introduce the word *instructions* to the children. Invite suggestions as to where they might find instructions, e.g. recipe book, instructions for playing a game, notices in the classroom or around the school, etc.

Read through the vocabulary strip with the children and ask them to suggest a caption for each picture, saying what must be done in as few words as possible. (See Sentence level work for emphasis on correct sentence structure and punctuation.)

Word level work

Ensure that the children can read and understand the words in the vocabulary strip on the poster. Use these as a starting point for a collection of 'themed' words on the topic of food, cooking or kitchens, which might include the names of utensils, foodstuffs and/or appliances. Invite suggestions from the class and record them on the board.

Select longer words from the themed list and play the 'hidden words' game introduced on page 39.

Sentence level work

Acting as scribe, ask the children to suggest some simple sentences that could be used to describe each of the stages illustrated on the poster. As previously, give priority to ensuring that they observe the need for a capital letter to begin each sentence and a full stop to complete it.

Invite the children to describe how they do a simple task, such as getting dressed or cleaning their teeth.

Inevitably, most sentences will begin with the personal pronoun *I*. Discuss the fact that *I* is special, as it always has a capital letter, whether it appears at the beginning of a sentence or not. Write the following sentences on the board, asking the children to correct your deliberate mistakes.

mum said i could have a lolly
i asked if i could have one for my friend
she said i could

Pupil's book

Text level work

Introduction

The pupil's book contains the same pictures as the poster, but this time with captions in the form of instructions.

If the poster has not been used, go through the teaching notes for the poster.

Read and investigate the 'style' of the instructions.

- The 'what you need' list.
  - Why do the children think it is necessary to have a list of the things needed?
- The instructions stating what to do.
- The verb at the beginning and the absence of a pronoun. Children should be able to identify the verb. They may more easily be able to understand the absence of a pronoun by thinking of instructions as sentences that don't say to whom they are addressed. Ask the children to follow this model and give some instructions that they may have heard from you, e.g.:

  Sit down quickly.
  Put your books away.
  Stand in a line.
- The order of the instructions.
  - Can they go in any order?
  - What difference would it make?
  - How does the order of the instructions help the reader?

Reading comprehension

Comprehension Copymaster 3 Non-fiction requires the children to identify literal information from the instructions, then select their favourite ice-lolly, draw and write about it.

The comprehension activity can be approached as a class discussion, in guided or independently working groups, or individually.

Word level work

Words within words

Play the 'hidden words' game (see page 39). Ask the children to find words in the passage that contain smaller words, e.g. *freezer* (*free, freeze*), *water* (*at, ate*).

Select long words from the 'environmental' text within the classroom and ask the children to copy each word and then find as many smaller words as possible within that word, e.g. *cupboard* (*cup, up, boar, board, a, oar*).

Word Skills Copymaster 3 Non-fiction provides practice with some of the irregular but significant words required in the early stages of independent writing.

The high-frequency words for this unit, to be taught as 'sight recognition' words, are as follows.

name
came
one
two
be

Sentence level work

Capital letters and full stops

Remind the children that *I* is a special word, as it always has a capital letter, whether it appears at the beginning of a sentence or not. Ask them to write a sentence about ice-lollies that includes the word *I*.

Text level work

Writing composition

Those children who are able should write their own simple instructions, which should include a 'You will need' list. Suggested topics are:

- Painting a picture
- Playing a game (agree with the children a particular game with which they are very familiar)
- Cleaning your teeth
- Making a jam sandwich.

For children who need more support, **Writing Copymaster 3 Non-fiction** is a picture and instruction matching exercise requiring children to cut out pictures and instructions and stick the pictures on a sheet of paper in the correct order, matched with the correct instructions. The children could be asked to write a 'You will need' list at the top of the sheet (i.e. fruit squash, a glass, water, a spoon).

Copymaster answers

Comprehension Copymaster 3

A 1 5
2 fruit squash, water, jug, ice-lolly mould, lolly sticks
3 4
4 mix pour put

B *Individual answers.*

unit 3

Word Skills Copymaster 3

A *Pupils trace and copy the words.*

B 1 Jenny said, "I want to make ice-lollies."
2 Mum said, "No, not today."
3 "Why don't you do a jigsaw," said Mum.
4 So Jenny did a jigsaw instead.

C *Pupils trace and copy the words.*

D If you come to my house today, we will make some ice-lollies.

Writing Copymaster 3

Individual answers.

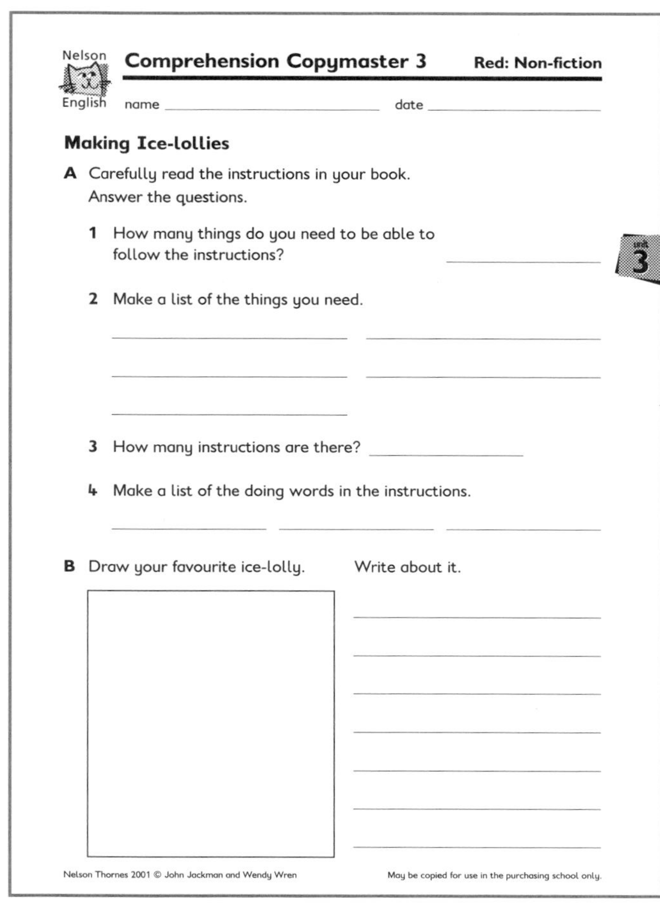

Nelson English **Comprehension Copymaster 3** **Red: Non-fiction**

name ______________________ date ______________________

Making Ice-lollies

A Carefully read the instructions in your book. Answer the questions.

1. How many things do you need to be able to follow the instructions? ______________
2. Make a list of the things you need.
3. How many instructions are there? ______________
4. Make a list of the doing words in the instructions.

B Draw your favourite ice-lolly. Write about it.

Nelson Thornes 2001 © John Jackman and Wendy Wren — May be copied for use in the purchasing school only.

unit 3

Nelson English **Word Skills Copymaster 3** **Red: Non-fiction**

name ______________________ date ______________________

Tricky Words

A Trace and copy the words.

1. to to to to ______ ______ ______
2. do do do do ______ ______ ______
3. no no no no ______ ______ ______
4. so so so so ______ ______ ______

B Write to or do or no or so in each sentence.

1. Jenny said, "I want ________ make ice-lollies."
2. Mum said, " ________ , not today."
3. "Why don't you ________ a jigsaw," said Mum.
4. ________ Jenny did a jigsaw instead.

C Trace and copy the words.

1. come come come ______ ______ ______
2. some some some ______ ______ ______

D Write come or some in each gap.

If you ________ to my house today, we will make ________ ice-lollies.

Nelson Thornes 2001 © John Jackman and Wendy Wren — May be copied for use in the purchasing school only.

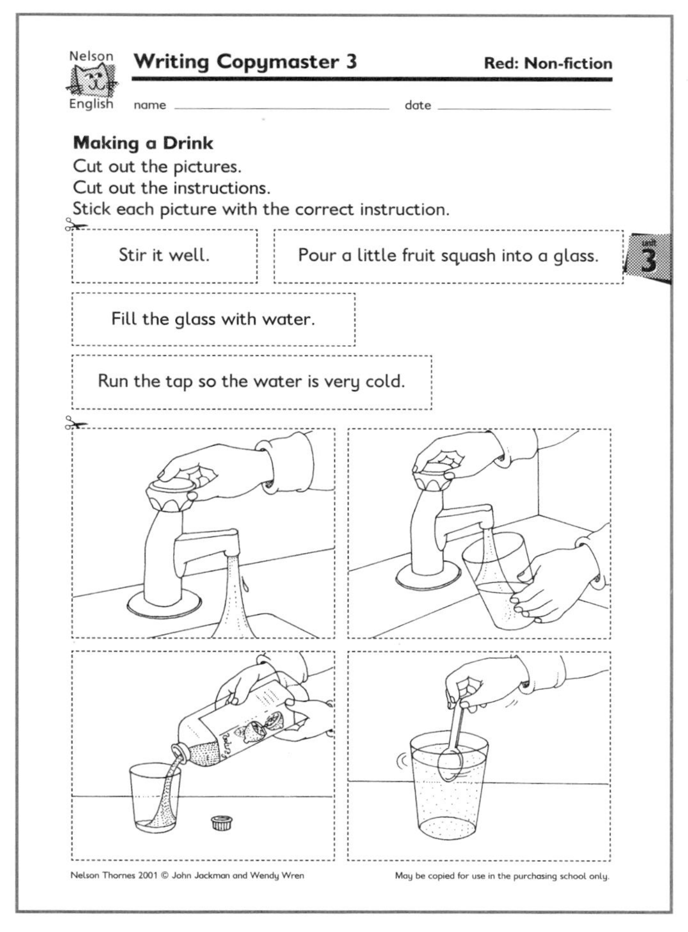

Nelson English **Writing Copymaster 3** **Red: Non-fiction**

name ______________________ date ______________________

Making a Drink

Cut out the pictures.
Cut out the instructions.
Stick each picture with the correct instruction.

Stir it well.

Pour a little fruit squash into a glass.

Fill the glass with water.

Run the tap so the water is very cold.

Nelson Thornes 2001 © John Jackman and Wendy Wren — May be copied for use in the purchasing school only.

The Gingerbread Man

Fiction

National Literacy Strategy

Year 1 Term 2

Range

Fiction: traditional stories

Pupils should be taught:

Text level work

Reading comprehension

4 to re-tell stories, giving the main points in sequence . . .;
7 to discuss reasons for, or causes of, incidents in stories;
8 to identify and discuss characters, e.g. appearance, behaviour, qualities; to speculate about how they might behave; to discuss how they are described in the text . . .;

Word level work

Phonological awareness, phonics and spelling

2 to investigate, read and spell words ending in *ff*, *ll*, *ss*, *ck*, *ng*;
3 . . . • to identify separate phonemes within words containing clusters in speech and writing;

Word recognition, graphic knowledge and spelling

6 to read on sight . . . high frequency words from Appendix List 1;

Sentence level work

Grammatical awareness

3 to predict words from preceding words in sentences and investigate the sorts of words that 'fit', suggesting appropriate alternatives, i.e. that make sense;

Text level work

Writing composition

14 to represent outlines of story plots using, e.g. captions, pictures, arrows to record main incidents in order, e.g. to make a class book, wall story, own version;
16 to use some of the elements of known stories to structure own writing.

Teaching Notes

Poster: Shared reading

Text level work

The poster shows the first four captioned pictures of the story of 'The Gingerbread Man'.

Begin by asking if any of the children are familiar with the story. Some children will probably have heard the story, so encourage them to piece it together orally for the rest of the class. If there is disagreement about the details, use the opportunity to explain that traditional tales such as 'The Gingerbread Man' and many well-known fairy tales, are very old and details change over time and through retelling.

Read the poster text to the children, pointing to the words as you read, and asking them to follow carefully.

Discuss what is happening in each picture. Ask the children to describe the physical appearance of each of the characters.

Discuss the two main incidents in the story, i.e.
(1) the gingerbread man runs away
(2) various characters shout "Stop!"

Base a discussion on the following points to concentrate the children's minds on character motive.

- Why do you think the old woman baked the gingerbread man?
- Why do you think he ran away?
- Why do you think everyone shouted at him to stop?
- Why do you think he did not stop?
- Just shouting "Stop!" did no good. If you were the old woman, what would you have done?

Word level work

Select some simple CVC words from the poster (e.g. *man, ran, did, can, not, boy, dog, cat*) and copy them on the board. Sound the letters clearly as you write them, inviting the children to join in with you. Highlight the phoneme (sound) that each letter represents. Next, write *stop* on the board. Talk about how the 's' and 't' are not sounded separately but together, as one sound.

Ask volunteers to offer other words beginning with 'st'. If appropriate, move on to words beginning with other letter clusters, e.g. 'sp'.

Examples of 'st-' words are:

stab stack stag stamp stand
stem step
stick stilts sting stink
stop stock
stub stuck stump stun stunk stunt

Examples of 'sp-' words are:

span spank spark spat
speck spell spend spent
spill spilt spin spit
spot
spun

Lists of simple words using blends or clusters can be found in the Nelson Spelling *Teacher's Book*.

Sentence level work

Display a simple sentence, covering a selected word. Invite the children to predict the missing word. Focus initially on obtaining clues from the preceding words but, later, all the words in a sentence can be used to help guess the missing word.

This task encourages useful and important predictive skills which enable children to 'read' words that might otherwise cause difficulty and, by experience, to gradually become aware of the grammatical features of a sentence. Realising that the word omitted is the name of a thing or person (noun) or the description of a thing or person (adjective) or an action word (verb) helps them to distinguish these categories of word. If children understand that each of these words can be varied by the writer to change the meaning of a sentence, they begin to appreciate the control that a writer has over his/her writing and the shades of meaning.

Pupil's book

Text level work

Introduction

The pupil's book contains almost the whole story of the gingerbread man in captioned pictures. The final picture is blank to encourage the children to predict the ending.

Read the captions to the children, encouraging them to follow in their books.

Discuss the character of the fox. Why do they think he offers to help? Do the children think the gingerbread man should trust him?

Discuss possible endings, for example:

- If the fox was a 'bad' character, he would eat the gingerbread man.
- If the fox was a 'good' character, he would take the gingerbread man safely across the river.
- If the fox was a friend of the old woman, he would take the gingerbread man to the old woman.

Ask the children how they would end the story.

Reading comprehension

Comprehension Copymaster 4 Fiction has two sections. Section A is a cloze activity requiring a literal response. Section B requires a personal response, suggesting an ending for the story. Section A can be approached as a class discussion, in guided or independently working groups, or individually.

Word level work

Words ending in 'ff', 'll', 'ss'

First, refer back to the Word level work based on the poster. Talk about the way some letters are sounded together. From the pupil's book, give the word *cross* as an example of a word with a double letter. Discuss how double letters might lead to spelling errors.

Write the following words on the board, and ask the children to read them and then sort and copy them into family groups according to the double letters:

stuff hill fluff fuss bell mess off
kiss pill

The following lists of simple double-letter words may be helpful for extending this work.

'-ff' words:

cliff sniff stiff
buff cuff gruff puff

'-ll' words:

fell sell smell spell swell tell well
yell
bill drill fill frill grill ill kill
mill skill spill still swill till
will
doll
gull hull skull

'-ss' words:

ass lass mass
bless dress less mess press stress
hiss miss
boss cross floss gloss moss toss

Use **Word Skills Copymaster 4 Fiction** for support.

The high-frequency words for this unit, to be taught as 'sight recognition' words, are as follows.

tree
seen
been
green
three

Sentence level work

Alternative words

Through discussion, help the children to realise that the sentences in the captions on page 15 are very similar, with just one word changed in each case. Ask them to write one, two or three of the sentences (as appropriate), altering one other word to change the meaning of each sentence, e.g. instead of *Stand* the child might offer *Sit* or *Lie*. Help the children to discover that they could change several of the words in each sentence, with varying effects on the meaning.

Text level work

Writing composition

The writing activity concentrates on narrative sequence, i.e. the order of events in a story. This can be tackled in a variety of ways.

Put the children into groups and give each group a different section of the story. On a large sheet of paper, each group should draw and caption their section of the story. One child from each group should come to the front with their section of the story and, through class discussion, the children arrange themselves in the correct order to tell the story.

Working individually, children could be asked to list the events of the story in narrative sequence. This may be ambitious for some children and **Writing Copymaster 4 Fiction** provides sentences for the pupils to join in the correct order. More able children could be asked to cut out the boxes on the copymaster, jumble them up and then stick them on a large sheet of paper in the correct order.

Copymaster answers

Comprehension Copymaster 4

A 1 The old <u>woman</u> made a gingerbread man.
2 When she opened the <u>oven</u> he jumped out.
3 The boy and the <u>girl</u> shouted at the gingerbread man.
4 The cat and the <u>dog</u> shouted at the gingerbread man.
5 The gingerbread man would not <u>stop</u>.
6 When the gingerbread man got to the <u>river</u> he could not cross.
7 The <u>fox</u> said he would help the gingerbread man.

B *Individual answers.*

Word Skills Copymaster 4

A

'ff' words	'ss' words	'll' words
off	cross	smell
puff	dress	sell
huff	fuss	tell

B 1 I can <u>smell</u> the gingerbread cooking.
2 Running made the gingerbread man <u>huff/puff</u> and <u>puff/huff</u>.
3 The fox helped the gingerbread man to <u>cross</u> the river.
4 He did not <u>tell</u> the gingerbread man he was going to eat him!

Writing Copymaster 4

Children should join the boxes in the correct order, to show the sequence of the story.

The Gingerbread Man

Run, run as fast as you can.
You can't stop me.
I'm the gingerbread man.

Stop!

An old woman made a gingerbread man.
She opened the oven door.
He jumped out and ran away.

"Stop!" said the old woman.
But he did not stop.
He ran and ran.

Stop!

Stop!

A boy said, "Stop!"
A girl said, "Stop!"
But he did not stop.
He ran and ran.

A cat said, "Stop!"
A dog said, "Stop!"
But he did not stop.
He ran and ran.

Nelson English

Red Level: Fiction

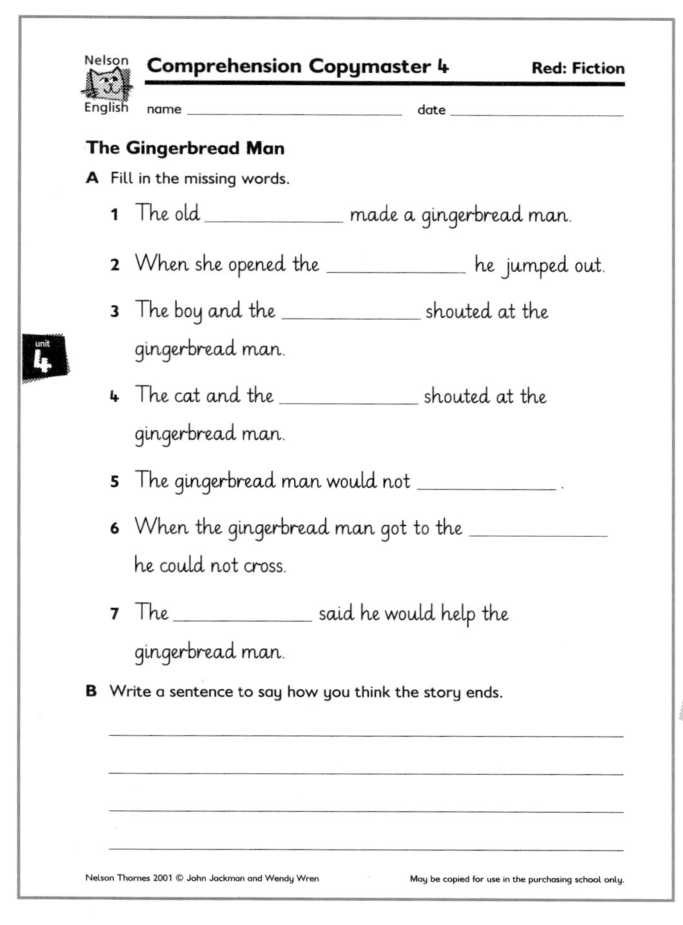

Nelson English

Comprehension Copymaster 4 — Red: Fiction

name ______________________ date ______________________

The Gingerbread Man

A Fill in the missing words.

1 The old ____________ made a gingerbread man.

2 When she opened the ____________ he jumped out.

3 The boy and the ____________ shouted at the gingerbread man.

4 The cat and the ____________ shouted at the gingerbread man.

5 The gingerbread man would not ____________ .

6 When the gingerbread man got to the ____________ he could not cross.

7 The ____________ said he would help the gingerbread man.

B Write a sentence to say how you think the story ends.

____

____

____

____

unit 4

unit 4

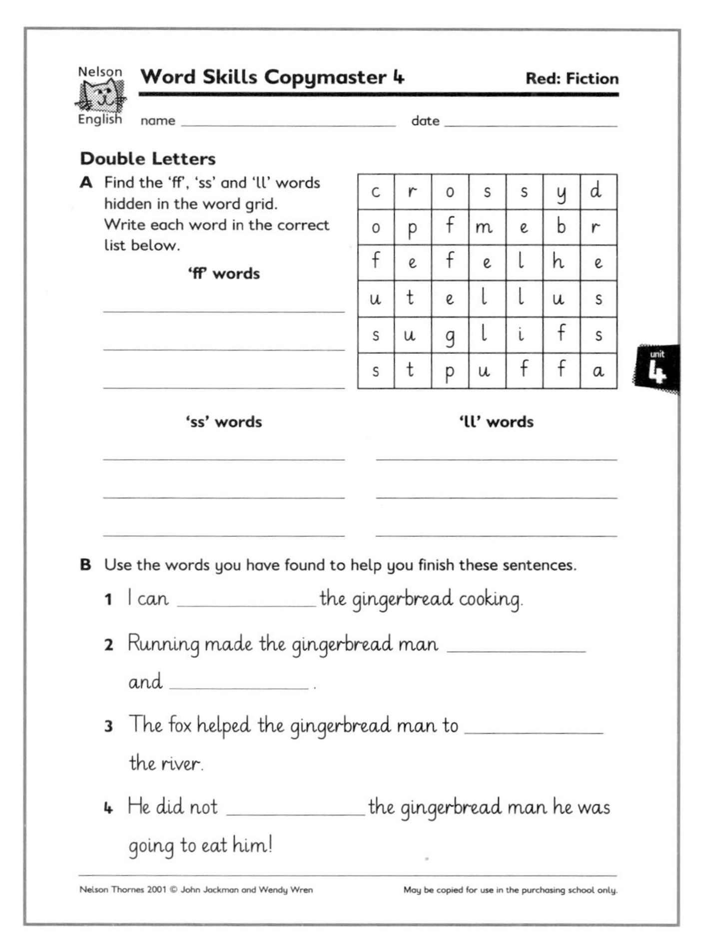

Nelson English

Word Skills Copymaster 4 — Red: Fiction

name ______________________ date ______________________

Double Letters

A Find the 'ff', 'ss' and 'll' words hidden in the word grid.
Write each word in the correct list below.

c	r	o	s	s	y	d
o	p	f	m	e	b	r
f	e	f	e	l	h	e
u	t	e	l	l	u	s
s	u	g	l	i	f	s
s	t	p	u	f	f	a

'ff' words

____

____

____

'ss' words

____

____

____

'll' words

____

____

____

B Use the words you have found to help you finish these sentences.

1 I can ____________ the gingerbread cooking.

2 Running made the gingerbread man ____________ and ____________ .

3 The fox helped the gingerbread man to ____________ the river.

4 He did not ____________ the gingerbread man he was going to eat him!

unit 4

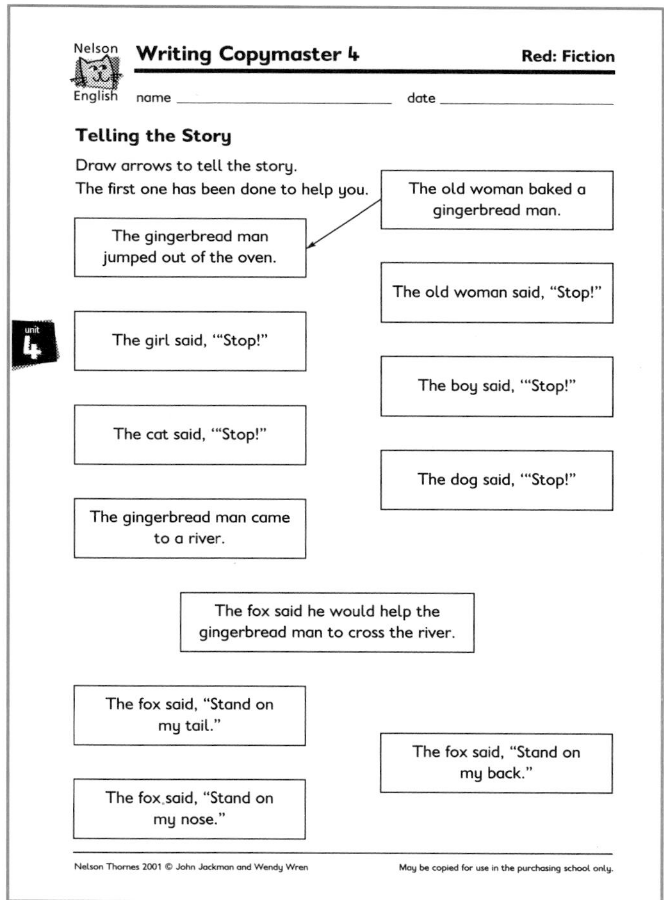

Nelson English

Writing Copymaster 4 — Red: Fiction

name ______________________ date ______________________

Telling the Story

Draw arrows to tell the story.
The first one has been done to help you.

The old woman baked a gingerbread man.

The gingerbread man jumped out of the oven.

The old woman said, "Stop!"

The girl said, '"Stop!"

The boy said, '"Stop!"

The cat said, '"Stop!"

The dog said, '"Stop!"

The gingerbread man came to a river.

The fox said he would help the gingerbread man to cross the river.

The fox said, "Stand on my tail."

The fox said, "Stand on my back."

The fox said, "Stand on my nose."

unit 4

All about Foxes

Non-fiction

National Literacy Strategy

Year 1 Term 2

Range

Non-fiction: information books, including non-chronological reports

Pupils should be taught:

Text level work

Reading comprehension

18 to read non-fiction books and understand that the reader doesn't need to go from start to finish but selects according to what is needed;

19 to predict what a given book might be about from a brief look at both front and back covers, including blurb, title, illustration; to discuss what it might tell in advance of reading and check to see if it does;

Word level work

Phonological awareness, phonics and spelling

2 to investigate, read and spell words ending in . . . *ck, ng*;

3
- to discriminate, read and spell words with final consonant clusters;
- to identify separate phonemes within words containing clusters in speech and writing; . . .
- to segment clusters into phonemes for spelling;

Sentence level work

Grammatical awareness

3 to predict words from preceding words in sentences and investigate the sorts of words that 'fit', suggesting appropriate alternatives, i.e. that make sense;

Text level work

Writing composition

25 to assemble information from own experience, e.g. food, pets; to use simple sentences to describe, based on reading; to write simple non-chronological reports; and to organise into lists, separate pages, charts.

Teaching Notes

Poster: Shared reading

Text level work

Introduce the subject of foxes to the children and ascertain:

- what they already know about foxes
- how they feel about foxes
- any stories/anecdotes they can tell you about foxes.

Display the poster and discuss with the children what is happening in each picture. Prompt them with such questions as:

Picture 1: What is the fox looking in?
Why do you think it is looking in the dustbin?

Picture 2: What do you think this fox is doing?

Picture 3: How old do you think these foxes are?
What are they doing?

Read through the vocabulary strip with the children and ask them to:

- suggest a caption for each picture
- describe one of the foxes
- suggest where foxes can be found.

Word level work

Revisit some of the letter clusters or blends used in the parallel Fiction unit (The Gingerbread Man). In particular, write *stop* on the board. Discuss the fact that words like these can be spelt incorrectly because the 'st' can be heard almost as one sound and careful listening is required to identify the individual letters.

Ask volunteers to suggest words in which the 'st' letter blend does not appear at the beginning.

Examples of '-st' words are:

best	nest	pest	rest	test	vest	west
fist	mist					
cost	lost					
bust	dust	just	must	rust		

If appropriate, move on to consider other blends or clusters that appear in the final position. Write on the board the word *hunt*, underlining 'nt'. Ask the children to sound these two letters, and discuss how they perform in a similar way to 'st' as discussed earlier. Examples of '-nt' words are:

ant	pant				
bent	lent	rent	sent	tent	went
hint	mint				
font					
hunt					

Sentence level work

As with the work in the parallel Fiction unit, give the children the opportunity to practise the important skill of predicting words from surrounding words and sentence grammar. Write a sentence, cover a suitable word and invite the children to predict what it is by reading the surrounding words.

This activity also gives children an opportunity to become aware of the grammatical features of a sentence by realising that the word omitted is, for example, the name of a thing or person (noun) or the description of a thing or person (adjective) or an action word (verb). This poster lends itself particularly to focusing on simple verb forms. Write on the board the opening of a simple sentence, such as: *The foxes are* _______. The children can then read the vocabulary strip and select suitable words to complete the sentence. Help the children to be aware that words that can be used to complete the sentence all tell us what the foxes are doing (verbs).

Pupil's book

Text level work

Introduction

Following on from the poster work, the pupil's book shows the front and back covers and some inside pages of a simple book about foxes.

Look at the front cover. Ask the children to identify:

- the title
- the author
- the illustration.

Look at the back cover. Explain to the children that the back cover of a book often provides more detailed information on what the book is about. The text on the back of a book is called the 'blurb'. Read through the blurb with the children and ask them what they would find out about if they read the book.

Read and discuss the pages from inside the fox book, asking the children what each page is about.

To help the children to understand that non-fiction books do not have to be read from cover to cover in the same way as stories, ask questions such as:

- If I wanted to know what foxes like to eat, which page should I read?
- If I wanted to know where foxes live, which pages should I read?
- If I wanted to know what foxes look like, which page should I read?

Discuss the illustrations with the children, identifying the various kinds, i.e. photographs, drawings, labelled diagrams.

Reading comprehension

Comprehension Copymaster 4 is in two sections. Section A requires the children to pick out literal information from the text. Section B reinforces the idea of looking for specific information on specific pages.

The comprehension questions can be approached as a whole-class discussion, in guided or independently working groups, or individually.

Word level work

Words ending in 'ck' and 'ng'

Although dealt with under the same objective in the NLS, there is scope for confusion when dealing with the letter combinations 'ck' and 'ng'. While 'ck' acts as a double consonant letter (similar to 'ff', 'll' and 'ss', which are covered in the parallel Fiction unit), 'ng' is actually a consonant digraph (similar to 'sh' or 'th'), in which the two letters acting together represent a sound quite different from two letters simply 'blended' together. For this reason, discretion will be needed as to whether the spelling of '-ng' words might better be postponed for some children. Note that, in English, the letters 'c' and 'k' are regular alternative spellings for the consonant sound /k/, as in cat and kid. Therefore, 'ck' is generally considered to be equivalent to a double-consonant grapheme.

Initially, draw to the children's attention the word *back* in the sentence *This is the back cover of the book about foxes.* (pupil's book, page 13). 'ck' words lend themselves conveniently to practising onset and rime patterns in the simple short-vowel context. Use the following list to encourage the children to realise that nearly all English words ending with the 'short c' sound, especially the simpler ones, are spelt with 'ck'.

back	lack	pack	rack	sack	tack
deck	neck	peck			
kick	lick	pick	sick	tick	wick
dock	lock	rock	sock		
duck	luck	muck	suck	tuck	

Words containing '-ng' can be separated into two main categories: those in which 'ng' is a phoneme within the root word, for example *bang*, and those in which 'ng' is part of a suffix, for example *sucking*. In both cases, help the children to hear the nasal 'ng' sound by writing on the board a selection of the following simple '-ng' words:

bang fang gang hang rang sang tang
ding king ping ring sing wing zing
dong gong long pong song
dung hung lung rung sung

This can be a convenient point at which to begin to introduce the reading and spelling of the suffix 'ing' to children who are ready. The following list will prove helpful, as it builds on the 'ck' words discussed earlier in this unit.

backing lacking packing racking sacking tacking
decking pecking
kicking licking picking ticking
docking locking rocking
ducking mucking sucking tucking

Word Skills Copymaster 4 provides support for work on '-ng' words and the addition of the suffix 'ing' to '-ng' words.

If you wish to extend this work to include more complex words with blends and digraphs incorporating the suffix 'ing', you might wish to refer to the Nelson Spelling *Teacher's Book*.

The high-frequency words for this unit, to be taught as 'sight recognition' words, are as follows.

how
now
down
this
that

Sentence level work

Alternative words

Following on from the Sentence level work in the parallel Fiction unit, invite the children to choose one of the sentences from the pages of the book about foxes in the pupil's book. Ask the children to write their chosen sentence so that it has a different meaning, by only altering one word. For example, in *Many foxes live in the country.*, *Many* might be replaced by *Some*, *No*, *Most*, etc.

Help the children to discover that, in some sentences, there may be more than one word that can be replaced with various other words, giving a different meaning each time.

Text level work

Writing composition

The writing objective can be tackled as follows:

- within the scope of current topic work from another curriculum area the children can use the knowledge they have gained to make simple captioned books;
- the children can work individually on a more general topic such as 'pets', producing a captioned drawing; the drawings can be collated to form a class book;
- with each child working individually on a simple topic such as 'My family', producing captioned pictures to form their own book.

Help the children to fold two sheets of A4 paper to form a very simple 'book', with a front cover, inner pages and a back cover.

Writing Copymaster 4 provides a front cover on which children add a title and illustration, and a back cover on which to write a simple blurb.

Copymaster answers

Comprehension Copymaster 1

A 1 Meet The Fox
2 Sam Tapp
3 in the country or in towns and cities
4 pointed
5 *two of the following:*
small animals, birds, insects, fruit

B 1 To find out where foxes live, I would read pages 4 and 5.
2 To find out what foxes look like, I would read page 6.
3 To find out what foxes eat, I would read page 7.

Word Skills Copymaster 1

A 1 ring 2 king 3 gong

B
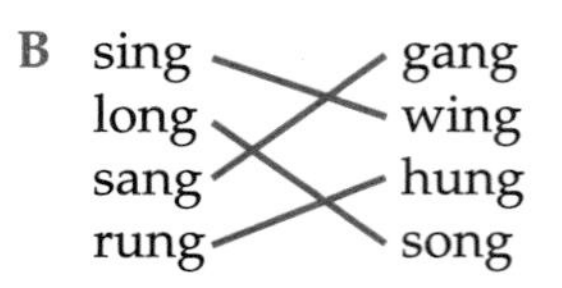

C 2 singing
3 hanging
4 clanging
5 ringing
6 stinging

Writing Copymaster 1

Individual answers.

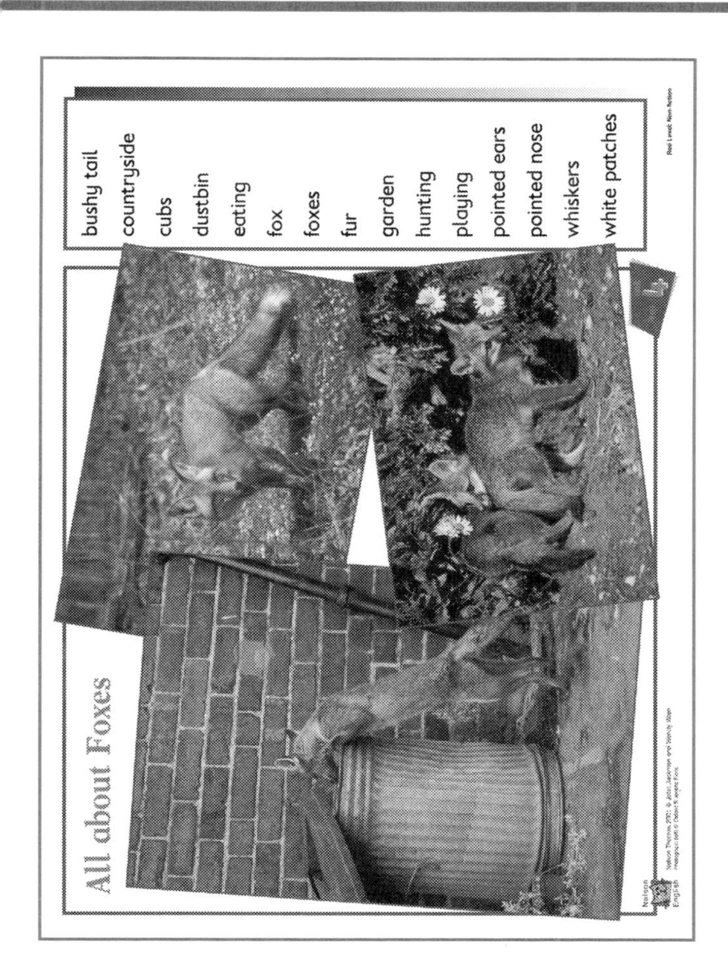

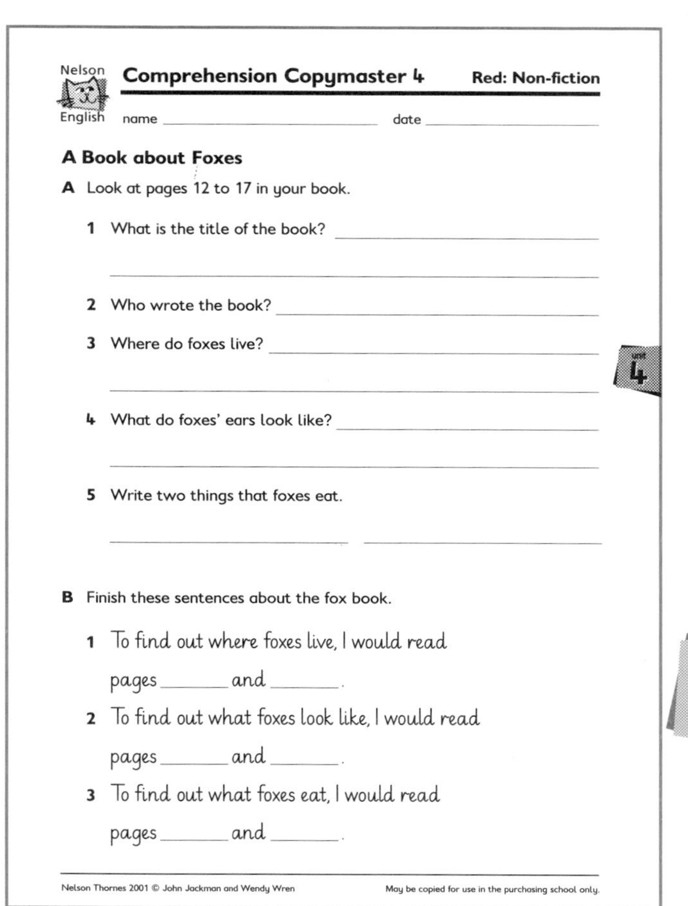
Nelson English

Comprehension Copymaster 4 **Red: Non-fiction**

name ______________ date ______________

A Book about Foxes

A Look at pages 12 to 17 in your book.

1 What is the title of the book? ______________

2 Who wrote the book? ______________

3 Where do foxes live? ______________

4 What do foxes' ears look like? ______________

5 Write two things that foxes eat.

______________ ______________

B Finish these sentences about the fox book.

1 To find out where foxes live, I would read pages ______ and ______.

2 To find out what foxes look like, I would read pages ______ and ______.

3 To find out what foxes eat, I would read pages ______ and ______.

unit 4

Nelson English

Word Skills Copymaster 4 **Red: Non-fiction**

name ______________ date ______________

'ng' Words

A Make the word to go with each picture.

1 r + ~~w~~ing = ______________

2 k + ~~s~~ing = ______________

3 g + ~~l~~ong = ______________

B Draw lines to join the words that rhyme.

sing	gang
long	wing
sang	hung
rung	song

C Sometimes we add 'ing' to an 'ng' word to show that something is happening now. For example: bring bringing

Now it has two 'ng's!

Add ing to these words.

The first one has been done to help you.

1 bang <u>banging</u> **2** sing ______________

3 hang ______________ **4** clang ______________

5 ring ______________ **6** sting ______________

Nelson English

Writing Copymaster 4 **Red: Non-fiction**

name ______________ date ______________

Book Cover

My Book about

If you read this book you will learn about:

Jack and the Beanstalk

Fiction

National Literacy Strategy

Year 1 Term 2

Range

Fiction: traditional stories . . . plays

Pupils should be taught:

Text level work

Reading comprehension

8 to identify and discuss characters, e.g. appearance, behaviour, qualities; to speculate about how they might behave; to discuss how they are described in the text; and to compare characters from different stories or plays;

9 to become aware of character and dialogue, e.g. by role-playing parts when reading aloud stories or plays with others;

Word level work

Phonological awareness, phonics and spelling

3 to discriminate, read and spell words with initial consonant clusters . . .:
- to identify separate phonemes within words containing clusters in speech and writing;
- to segment clusters into phonemes for spelling;

Word recognition, graphic knowledge and spelling

6 to read on sight . . . high frequency words identified for Year 1 . . . from Appendix List 1;

Sentence level work

Sentence construction and punctuation

5 to continue demarcating sentences in writing, ending a sentence with a full stop;

6 to use the term *sentence* appropriately to identify sentences in text, i.e. those demarcated by capital letters and full stops;

Text level work

Writing composition

15 to build simple profiles of characters from stories read, describing characteristics, appearances, behaviour with pictures, single words, captions, words and sentences from text;

16 to use some of the elements of known stories to structure own writing.

Teaching Notes

Poster: Shared reading

Text level work

The poster shows a prose version of the beginning of the story of Jack and the beanstalk, which also forms the basis of the play script in the pupil's book.

Begin by asking if any of the children are familiar with the story of Jack and the beanstalk. Some children will probably have heard the story, so encourage them to piece it together orally for the rest of the class. As with Unit 4 Fiction (The Gingerbread Man), if there is disagreement about the details, use the opportunity to discuss the way in which traditional tales change over time.

Read the poster text aloud, pointing to the words as you read and asking the children to follow carefully.

Discuss the incidents in the story, asking the children to help you compile a list which reflects the narrative sequence, i.e. what happens when:

- Jack's mother calls him and tells him to sell the cow
- Jack sets off for market with the cow
- he meets an old man on the road
- the old man offers Jack magic beans for the cow
- Jack takes the beans home to his mother

Base a discussion on the following points to concentrate the children's minds on character motive.

- Why did Jack's mother want to sell the cow?
- How do you think Jack felt about selling the cow?
- Why do you think the old man wanted the cow?
- Do you think it was a good idea to swap the cow for some magic beans?
- What do you think Jack's mother will do?

Word level work

Remind the children of the initial letter clusters taught in earlier units, i.e. 'st-' and 'sp-' (Unit 4).

Point out words on the poster, that begin with a blend which includes the letter 'l' (i.e. *black, glum, plant*). Copy the words on the board. Underline the 'bl', 'gl' or 'pl' at the beginning of each word, noting the 'l', which is common to all. Explain that many words beginning with pairs of letters (clusters or blends) include an 'l' as the second letter. Then write the following words on the board:

flag plot slam blot clap

Ask the children to suggest other words that sound as though they might begin with the same initial cluster of letters. Encourage them to help you spell their suggestions by carefully sounding out each phoneme in each word offered.

The following lists of words may be helpful for extending this work. A more extensive selection of simple words incorporating blends or clusters can be found in the Nelson Spelling *Teacher's Book*.

'fl-' words:
flag flan flap flat
flick fling flip
flock flog flop

'pl-' words:
plan plank
plod plot
pluck plug plum plus

'sl-' words:
slack slab slam slap
slick slid slim slip slit
slot
slug slum

'bl-' words:
bled
block blob blot

'cl-' words:
clan clap
click clip
clock clog clot
club cluck

'gl-' words:
glad
glum

Sentence level work

When looking in detail at the poster text, draw attention to the various punctuation marks, a variety of which are represented on the poster. Revise the notion of a full stop ending a sentence by asking a volunteer to show where one of the sentences ends. Ask how they know. Ask another child (who might otherwise have had difficulty) to point to a full stop and tell you what it means.

Someone might ask about the exclamation marks and question marks that appear in this extract. Without going into too much detail, explain that these are also used to tell a reader that a sentence (a special type of sentence) has finished – as is indicated by the full stop that each of these punctuation marks has 'built into' it.

Pupil's book

Text level work

Introduction

The text in the pupil's book is based on that on the poster, but is presented in the form of a play script.

Read the play script to the children, encouraging them to follow in their books.

Ensure the poster is displayed and discuss the difference between the poster version and the pupil's book version of the story, i.e.:

layout
dialogue
scenes
stage directions.

Put the children into groups of three and allow them time to practise presenting the play, helping them to learn their lines. Encourage the children to think about how certain lines will be spoken to show how a particular character was feeling at the time, e.g.:

JACK: Sell the cow! Sell Daisy the cow! (*upset/horrified*)
MOTHER: Beans! We needed money to get food! ... etc. (*angry; anxious*)

Reading comprehension

Comprehension Copymaster 5 Fiction has two sections. Section A is a cloze activity requiring a literal response. Section B requires a personal response, choosing a favourite character. Section A can be approached as a class discussion, in guided or independently working groups, or individually.

Word level work

Double letters and 'ck'

This unit offers the opportunity to reinforce earlier work on double letters and 'ck' words. Remember that, as noted previously, the letters 'c' and 'k' are regular alternative spellings for the consonant sound /k/ as in *cat* and *kid*. Therefore, 'ck' is generally considered to be equivalent to a double-consonant grapheme.

First, remind the children about the way that some letters 'work together'. Then, from the text in the pupil's book, choose an example of a double-letter word (e.g. *sell, will*) and use *Jack* as an example of 'ck' acting as a double letter. Write the words on the board and ask the children to copy them, and write a rhyming word next to each, for example:

sell	bell	fell	smell	spell	swell	tell
	well	yell				
will	bill	drill	fill	frill	grill	hill
	ill	kill	mill	pill	skill	spill
	still	mill	till			
Jack	back	black	crack	hack	lack	pack
	rack	sack	smack	snack	stack	tack

Continue the work with other 'ck' and double-letter words, examples of which can be found in the Nelson Spelling *Teacher's Book*.

Use **Word Skills Copymaster 5 Fiction** for support with 'ck' words.

The high-frequency words for this unit, to be taught as 'sight recognition' words, are as follows.

what
when
where
who
if

Sentence level work

Recognising sentences

On the board, write a sentence from the pupil's book, e.g. *Come on, Daisy*. Ask a volunteer to say how we know that this is a sentence, i.e. it has a capital letter at the beginning and a full stop at the end.

Then write on the board some phrases (i.e. not sentences, so without capital letters and full stops) and a sentence or two and ask the children to identify which are the sentences.

When you are confident that the class/group has grasped the significance of capital (upper case) letters and full stops, ask those that are able to copy one sentence from the pupil's book.

Text level work

Writing composition

The writing activity concentrates on building character profiles of Jack, Jack's mother and the old man.

Put the children into groups and give each group a different character. By photocopying and cutting out the relevant picture from **Writing Copymaster 5 Fiction**, ensure that each group has a picture of their character stuck into the middle of a large sheet of paper.

Ask the groups to use the illustrations in the pupil's book and on the poster to help them write words and phrases around the picture of their character to describe what they look like, for example:

Jack: skinny, blonde hair, scruffy, big feet, red hat, etc.

Be on hand to help with spelling.

Discuss with each group what kind of person they think their character is. They can add any useful descriptive words to the physical description they have already written, for example:

Jack – kind, obedient, foolish.

Again, be on hand to help with spelling.

The children can then colour their pictures to match the physical description. Display groups' work and discuss how similarly/differently the various groups saw their character's personality.

Copymaster answers

Comprehension Copymaster 5

A 1 Jack's mother wanted him to sell the cow.
2 Jack was on the way to market when he met an old man.
3 The old man gave Jack some magic beans.
4 Jack ran to tell his mother about the beans.
5 Jack's mother was cross.
6 She threw the beans out of the window.

B *Individual answers.*

Word Skills Copymaster 5

A 2 click
3 flick
4 block
5 smack
6 trick
7 smock
8 cluck
9 pluck
10 black
11 track
12 slack

B 2 clock
3 crack
4 brick
5 stack
6 truck
7 stick
8 flock

Writing Copymaster 5

Individual answers.

Jack and the Beanstalk

Once upon a time there was a boy called Jack. He lived with his mother. They were very poor.

One day, Jack's mother said to him, "Jack, we have no food to eat. You will have to take the cow and sell her."

"Sell Daisy the cow!" cried Jack.

"We need money for food," said his mother.

Jack took the old black cow down the road to the market. On the way, Jack saw an old man.

"Where are you going?" asked the old man.

"I have to sell the cow," said Jack. He felt glum.

"You give me the cow and I will give you these magic beans," said the old man.

"What can I do with them?" asked Jack.

"Plant them and you will see," said the old man.

Jack gave the old man the cow and took the beans. He ran home to tell his mother.

Red Level: Fiction 5

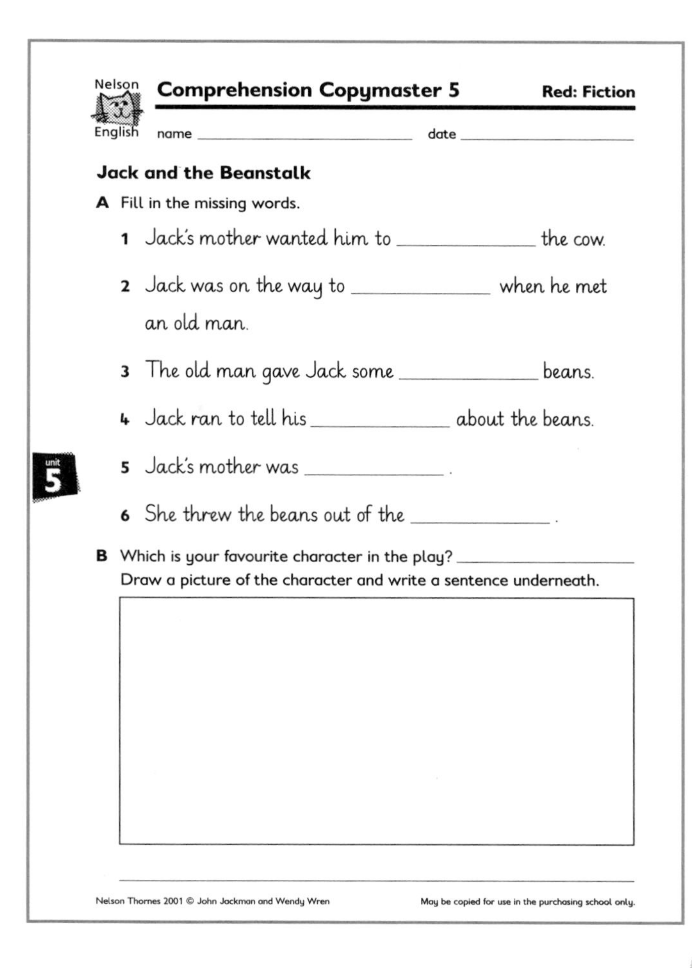

Nelson English **Comprehension Copymaster 5** **Red: Fiction**

name ______________ date ______________

Jack and the Beanstalk

A Fill in the missing words.

1 Jack's mother wanted him to __________ the cow.

2 Jack was on the way to __________ when he met an old man.

3 The old man gave Jack some __________ beans.

4 Jack ran to tell his __________ about the beans.

5 Jack's mother was __________ .

6 She threw the beans out of the __________ .

B Which is your favourite character in the play? __________

Draw a picture of the character and write a sentence underneath.

Nelson Thornes 2001 © John Jackman and Wendy Wren — May be copied for use in the purchasing school only.

unit 5

Nelson English **Word Skills Copymaster 5** **Red: Fiction**

name ______________ date ______________

'ck' Words

A Do these word sums.
The first one has been done to help you.

1 s + tuck =	stuck	2 c + lick =	______
3 f + lick =	______	4 b + lock =	______
5 s + mack =	______	6 t + rick =	______
7 s + mock =	______	8 c + luck =	______
9 p + luck =	______	10 b + lack =	______
11 t + rack =	______	12 s + lack =	______

B Add the missing letter, then write the word underneath.
The first one has been done for you.

1 tr i ck — trick
2 cl __ ck
3 cr __ ck
4 br __ ck
5 st __ ck
6 tr __ ck
7 st __ ck
8 fl __ ck

Nelson Thornes 2001 © John Jackman and Wendy Wren — May be copied for use in the purchasing school only.

Nelson English **Writing Copymaster 5** **Red: Fiction**

name ______________ date ______________

Jack and the Beanstalk

Nelson Thornes 2001 © John Jackman and Wendy Wren — May be copied for use in the purchasing school only.

Growing Beans

Non-fiction

National Literacy Strategy

Year 1 Term 2

Range

Non-fiction: information books, including non-chronological reports

Pupils should be taught:

Text level work

Reading comprehension

17 to use terms 'fiction' and 'non-fiction', noting some of their differing features, e.g. layout, titles, contents page, use of pictures, labelled diagrams;

Word level work

Phonological awareness, phonics and spelling

3
- to discriminate, read and spell words with final consonant clusters . . .;
- to identify separate phonemes within words containing clusters in speech and writing;
- to segment clusters into phonemes for spelling;

Word recognition, graphic knowledge and spelling

6 to read on sight . . . high frequency words identified for Year 1 . . . from Appendix List 1;

Sentence level work

Sentence construction and punctuation

5 to continue demarcating sentences in writing, ending a sentence with a full stop;

6 to use the term *sentence* appropriately to identify sentences in text, i.e. those demarcated by capital letters and full stops;

Text level work

Writing composition

22 to write labels for drawings and diagrams, e.g. growing beans, . . .;

23 to produce extended captions, e.g. to explain paintings in wall displays or to describe artefacts.

Teaching Notes

Poster: Shared reading

Text level work

Discuss the idea of planting seeds and growing plants. Have the children ever grown anything, e.g. mustard and cress, sunflowers, etc.? Did the plants grow well? Did they die? What do plants need in order to grow?

Display the poster and discuss what each picture shows, i.e.:

Picture 1: children planting seeds
Picture 2: a small shoot appearing above the soil and a root system beginning to develop; plant being watered
Picture 3: much bigger bean plants with flowers and leaves; some of the flowers having turned into small beans
Picture 4: children picking beans from a fully developed bean plant.

Prompt discussion with such questions as:

Picture 1: What are the children doing?
Picture 2: What can you see above the soil? What can you see below the soil?
Picture 3: What do the plants look like now?
Picture 4: What are the children picking?

Read through the vocabulary strip on the poster with the children and ask them to use the words to suggest a caption for each picture.

Do the children think it is important for the pictures to be in the order they appear, or would any order do? Lead the children to see that information needs to be organised carefully so the reader can follow what is happening.

Compare the poster with that from the parallel fiction unit (Jack and the Beanstalk) to investigate, in simple terms, the difference between 'fiction' and 'non-fiction'. It is sufficient at this stage for the children to grasp that a piece of fiction is essentially a 'story' and non-fiction text gives us information. This could be extended/reinforced by investigating the differences between a selection of fiction and non-fiction books.

Word level work

Refresh the children's memories about the initial letter clusters taught in the parallel fiction unit, i.e. 'l' blends.

Next, revise the previously taught clusters that appear at the end of words, i.e. '-ck' and '-ng' (Unit 4 Fiction), '-ng', '-st' and '-nt' (Unit 4 Non-fiction), '-ck' (Unit 5 Fiction). Ask the children to suggest examples of each. These can be written on the board and then read aloud together.

Another important group of words share the '-nd' final cluster. Write on the board words that share the '-nd' final cluster, e.g. *wind*, *bend*. Ask the children to suggest other '-nd' words, for example:

and band hand land sand stand
end bend blend lend mend send
bind find kind mind wind
bond fond pond
fund

If appropriate, the work might be extended to consider other frequent final clusters, such as '-mp', for example:

camp clamp damp lamp ramp stamp
imp limp
bump dump hump jump lump pump slump stump
romp

Use **Word Skills Copymaster 5 Non-fiction** for support.

Sentence level work

Acting as scribe, ask the children to dictate a sentence about the poster. Write it on the board without the capital letter and full stop. Invite suggestions about the mistakes you have made. Possibly invite a volunteer to correct your errors. Then invite suggestions for another sentence. This time, write it correctly, and invite a child to circle the two things that show it is a complete sentence (capital letter and full stop).

Pupil's book

Text level work

Introduction

Following on from the poster, the pupil's book shows labelled photographs of bean plants growing. Discuss what is shown in the photographs and read the labels.

Using the poster for reference, for each picture ask the children what has to have happened before the plant has reached the stage pictured, and what will happen after this stage.

Reading comprehension

Comprehension Copymaster 5 Non-fiction part A requires the children to 'read' the photographs for literal vocabulary and complete sentences using words from a word box. Part B requires children to use vocabulary from the poster and pupil's book to label a simple diagram of a bean plant.

The comprehension activity can be approached as a class discussion, in guided or independently working groups, or individually

Word level work

Important words

Given the largely non-textual nature of the pupils' material in this unit, it is suggested that now is a good opportunity to work on the key groups of words suggested in Appendix List 1 of the NLS document: the months of the year (which can be related to when beans are planted, grow and can be picked), common colour words and number words to twenty.

The high-frequency words for this unit, to be taught as 'sight recognition' words, are as follows.

out
about
here
there
saw

Sentence level work

Using capital letters for names

Following on from the Word level work above, ask if anyone has noticed anything special about the way we write the names of the months of the year. Discuss the fact that we give capital (upper case) letters to special words like this, even if they aren't the first word in a sentence. Ask for further examples (e.g. the days of the week, special days such as religious festivals, names of countries, etc.). Focus on the children's own names, as this reinforces the 'special' name concept. Extend this to the name of your local town or village, school, etc. In each case, write the word on the board without the capital letter and invite the children to spot your mistake.

Text level work

Writing composition

The writing objective requires the children to write labels and captions. Part B of the Comprehension Copymaster involves labelling a diagram. **Writing Copymaster 5 Non-fiction** illustrates the four stages of growing a bean plant which appear on the poster, and children are required to caption them.

Ensure that the poster is displayed and encourage the children to use both the vocabulary strip on the poster and the labels in the pupil's book to help them. If children are still writing only one or two words for captions, help them to form simple sentences to describe what is happening in each picture.

Copymaster answers

Comprehension Copymaster 5

A 1 The bean has grown from a seed.
2 The bean plant has roots in the soil.
3 The bean plant has green leaves.
4 The bean plant has red flowers.
5 There are some small beans growing on the plant.

B *Children should correctly label the root, soil, seed, leaf and stem.*

Word Skills Copymaster 5

A 1 hand
2 bend
3 band

B
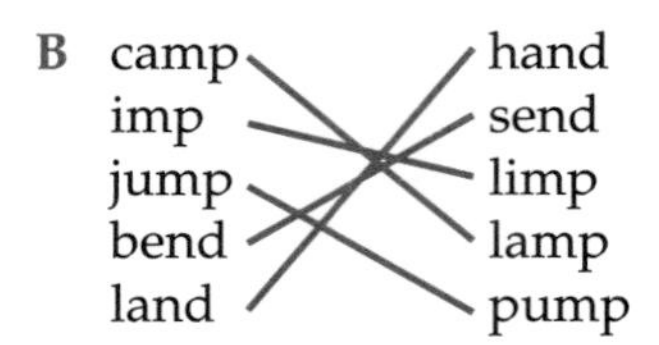

D 2 stamping
3 sending
4 landing
5 standing
6 mending

Writing Copymaster 5

Individual answers.

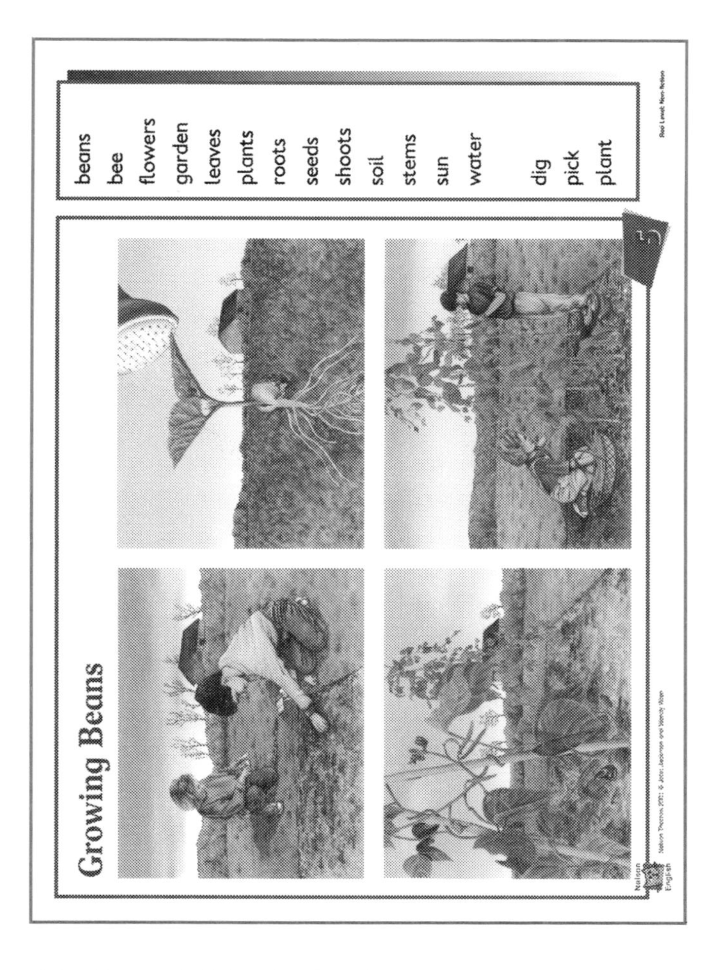

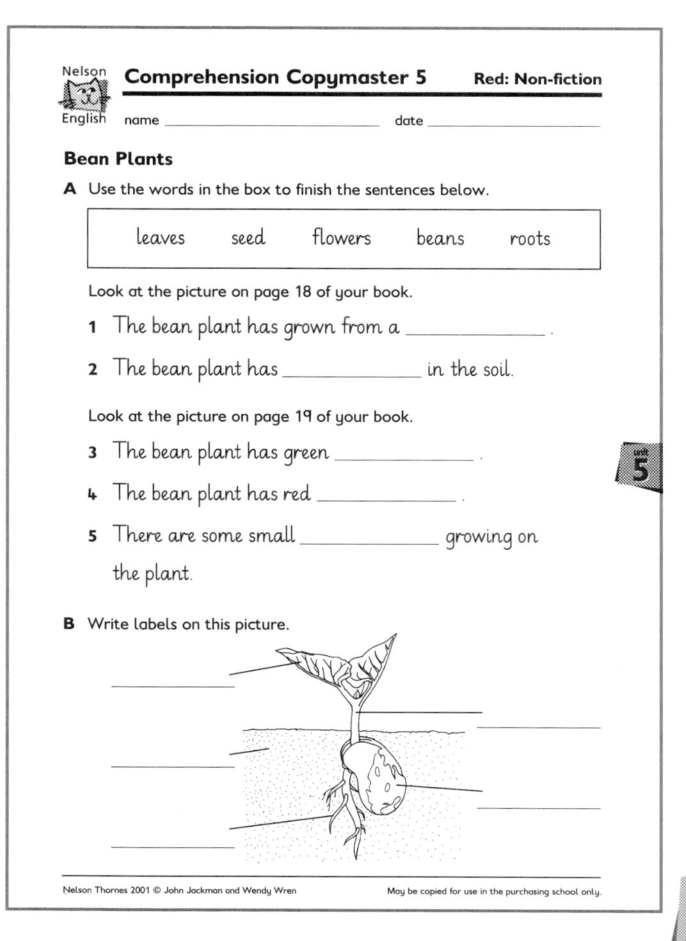
Nelson English

Comprehension Copymaster 5 — Red: Non-fiction

name ______________________ date ______________________

Bean Plants

A Use the words in the box to finish the sentences below.

leaves	seed	flowers	beans	roots

Look at the picture on page 18 of your book.

1 The bean plant has grown from a ______________ .

2 The bean plant has ______________ in the soil.

Look at the picture on page 19 of your book.

3 The bean plant has green ______________ .

4 The bean plant has red ______________ .

5 There are some small ______________ growing on the plant.

B Write labels on this picture.

Nelson Thornes 2001 © John Jackman and Wendy Wren — May be copied for use in the purchasing school only.

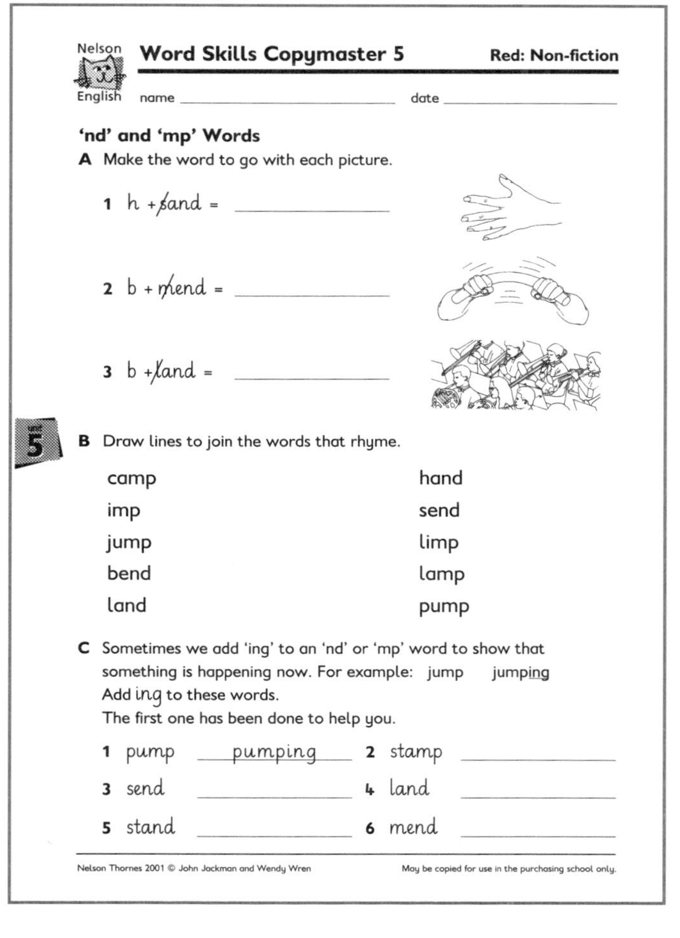
Nelson English

Word Skills Copymaster 5 — Red: Non-fiction

name ______________________ date ______________________

'nd' and 'mp' Words

A Make the word to go with each picture.

1 h + sand = ______________

2 b + mend = ______________

3 b + land = ______________

B Draw lines to join the words that rhyme.

camp	hand
imp	send
jump	limp
bend	lamp
land	pump

C Sometimes we add 'ing' to an 'nd' or 'mp' word to show that something is happening now. For example: jump jumping
Add ing to these words.
The first one has been done to help you.

1 pump pumping 2 stamp ______________

3 send ______________ 4 land ______________

5 stand ______________ 6 mend ______________

Nelson Thornes 2001 © John Jackman and Wendy Wren — May be copied for use in the purchasing school only.

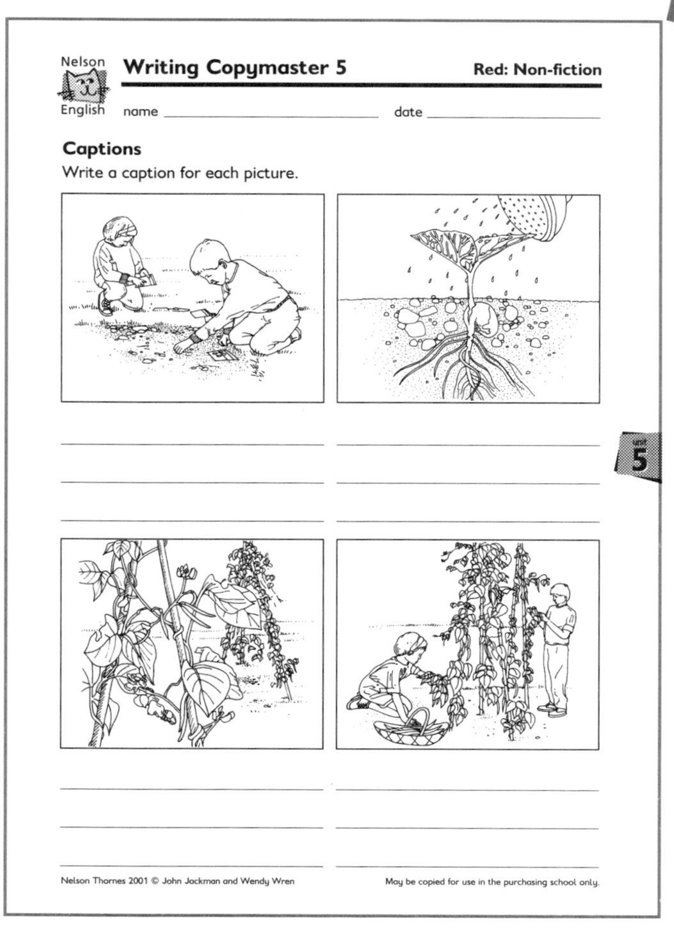
Nelson English

Writing Copymaster 5 — Red: Non-fiction

name ______________________ date ______________________

Captions

Write a caption for each picture.

Toys unit 6

Teddy Bear

Fiction

National Literacy Strategy

Year 1 Term 2

Range

Fiction: poems with familiar, predictable and patterned language . . . including . . . action verses and rhymes

Pupils should be taught:

Text level work

Reading comprehension

11 to learn and recite simple poems and rhymes, with actions, and to re-read them from the text;

Word level work

Word recognition, graphic knowledge and spelling

7 to recognise the critical features of words, e.g. length, common spelling patterns and words within words;

8 to investigate and learn spellings of words with 's' for plurals;

9 to read on sight . . . high frequency words identified for Year 1 . . . from Appendix List 1;

Sentence level work

Grammatical awareness

3 to predict words from preceding words in sentences and investigate the sorts of words that 'fit', suggesting appropriate alternatives, i.e. that make sense;

Sentence construction and punctuation

5 to continue demarcating sentences in writing, ending a sentence with a full stop;

6 to use the term *sentence* appropriately to identify sentences in text, i.e. those demarcated by capital letters and full stops;

7 to use capital letters for the personal pronoun '*I*' . . . and for the start of a sentence;

Text level work

Writing composition

13 to substitute and extend patterns from reading through language play, e.g. by using same lines and introducing new words, extending rhyming or alliterative patterns, adding further rhyming words, lines.

Teaching Notes

Poster: Shared reading

Text level work

The poster shows the first verse of the action poem 'Teddy Bear'.

Discuss teddy bears with the children. Prompt them with questions such as:

- Do you have a teddy bear?
- Is it your only/favourite cuddly toy?
- What is it called?
- How long have you had it?
- Does it go everywhere with you/stay in your room?
- Is the teddy bear your favourite toy?
- If not, which is your favourite toy?
- Why?

Read the poem to the children, pointing to the words as you read, and asking them to follow carefully.

Ask the children to mime the actions of the poem while you read it again. Work towards the children reciting the poem and doing the actions at the same time.

Can they pick out the rhyming words? Can they think of any other words that rhyme with *nose/toes* and *ground/around* or other rhyming pairs that could be used in the poem (e.g. *chin/shin*, *chair/hair*, *head/bed*)?

Word level work

Play the 'hidden words' game first introduced in Unit 3 Fiction (see page 39). Ask a volunteer to point to the word *your* on the poster. Write *your* on the board. Ask for suggestions as to any small words that might be found 'hiding' in it (i.e. *you*, *our*).

Follow a similar approach with other words on the poster, e.g. *bear* (*be*, *ear*), *touch* (*to*, *ouch*), *nose* (*no*), *toes* (*to*, *toe*), *ground* (*round*), *turn* (*urn*).

As appropriate, repeat the activity with words from the list of high-frequency words in Appendix List 1 of the NLS, for example, *another*, *brother*, *called*, *down*, *made*, *once*, *some*, *their*, *water*, *what*, *when*, *where*, *your*. Encourage the children to learn to spell the words at the same time. This activity will be more effective if not too many words are undertaken at a time.

Sentence level work

Earlier units included activities in which children predicted missing words in sentences. These were largely driven by the implied grammatical structure of the sentence. In poetry, where the rhyme is strong, the children can enjoy the fun of predicting likely 'correct' words from a range of rhyming alternatives.

Cover the word *toes* on the poster. On the board, write *shoes*, *toes*, *legs*, *feet*. Read the words aloud with the children. Then read the first four lines of the poem, using each of the four alternatives in turn in the gap where *toes* was. Ask for suggestions as to which word 'fits' best. Discuss why this is (i.e. rhyme). Repeat with lines 5 to 8 of the poem, covering *around* and filling the gap with *over*, *inside-out* and *upside-down*, again discussing which fits best and why.

From this, develop some other simple rhyming couplets, with the children predicting the second rhyming word, e.g.

Teddy bear,
Teddy bear, sit on the seat,
Now lean over
and touch your _____. (*feet*)

Some children may be able to offer other couplets of their own.

Discuss and list other words that could be used in the poem, working towards the children writing a new verse for the poem, e.g.:

Teddy bear,
Teddy bear, touch your <u>cheek</u>.
Teddy bear,
Teddy bear, take a <u>peek</u>,
Teddy bear,
Teddy bear, <u>jump up high</u>,
Teddy bear,
Teddy bear, <u>touch the sky</u>.

Pupil's book

Text level work

Introduction

Both verses of the poem 'Teddy Bear' can be found in the pupil's book.

Read the complete poem with the children and, if the poster has not been used, go through the teacher's notes and activities for the poster, which relate to the first verse.

Give the children the opportunity to:

- recite the poem
- recite the poem and do the actions
- pick out the rhyming words
- substitute words in the second verse of the poem.

Reading comprehension

Part A of **Comprehension Copymaster 6 Fiction** requires the children to pick out literal information from the poem. In part B, they are asked to draw and write about Teddy Bear doing another action. The writing can vary from a simple caption to several sentences, depending on individual ability. Section A can be approached as a class discussion, in guided or independently working groups, or individually.

Word level work

Plurals

Spend a little time ensuring that the children are comfortable with the notion of *plural* meaning 'more than one'. At your discretion, some or all of the children might be encouraged to use the terms *singular* and *plural*.

Work on plurals offers the opportunity to meet the NLS objective for Year 1 that pupils learn to recognise and spell the number words to 20.

Write on the board the following words, which are taken from the poem: *toes*, *stairs*, *prayers*. Ask a volunteer to read the words aloud. Write a number word (e.g. *five*) in front of each word, for example, *five toes*, *four stairs*, *three prayers*. Next, rub out the number words and replace each with *one*. Ask for suggestions as to what other changes are now required (i.e. removing the 's' from each word).

Write on the board a list of other singular words whose plurals are made by the simple addition of 's'. Then write a number word (two or above) in front of each word and invite volunteers in turn to come forward and add the missing 's' to one of the words.

Use **Word Skills Copymaster 6 Fiction** for support.

The high-frequency words for this unit, to be taught as 'sight recognition' words, are as follows.

then
than
may
way
jump

Sentence level work

Recognising sentences and using 'I'

Having read the poem together, ask a child to say what they like best about the poem. Acting as scribe, write *I like the poem because* ________. Ask for a suggestion to complete the sentence. Point out that *I* is a small word referring to themselves, which always has a capital (or upper case) letter, as would their name.

Give the beginning of another sentence, such as *The toy I like best is* ___________. Help the children to complete it for themselves, paying particular attention to the upper case *I*.

Text level work

Writing composition

Following on from the poster and pupil's book discussion, the children should write their own poem using 'Teddy Bear' as the model. For children who need support, **Writing Copymaster 6 Fiction** provides a framework, with picture clues, requiring children to fill in words to complete a new verse of the poem.

Copymaster answers

Comprehension Copymaster 6

A 1 toes nose ground
2 turn around
3 says his prayers
4 put out the light

B *Individual answers.*

Word Skills Copymaster 6

A *Children draw lines to connect the correct number, word and picture.*

B 1 two bears
2 three bikes
3 four dolls
4 five boats

Writing Copymaster 6

Teddy Bear,
Teddy Bear, wash your ~~face~~.
Teddy Bear,
Teddy Bear, tie your ~~lace~~.
Teddy Bear,
Teddy Bear, ~~jump~~ about.
Teddy Bear,
Teddy Bear, sing and ~~shout~~.

Teddy Bear

Do the same actions as Teddy!

Teddy bear,
Teddy bear, touch your nose,
Teddy bear,
Teddy bear, touch your toes,
Teddy bear,
Teddy bear, touch the ground,
Teddy bear,
Teddy bear, turn around.

Nelson English

Red Level: Fiction

6

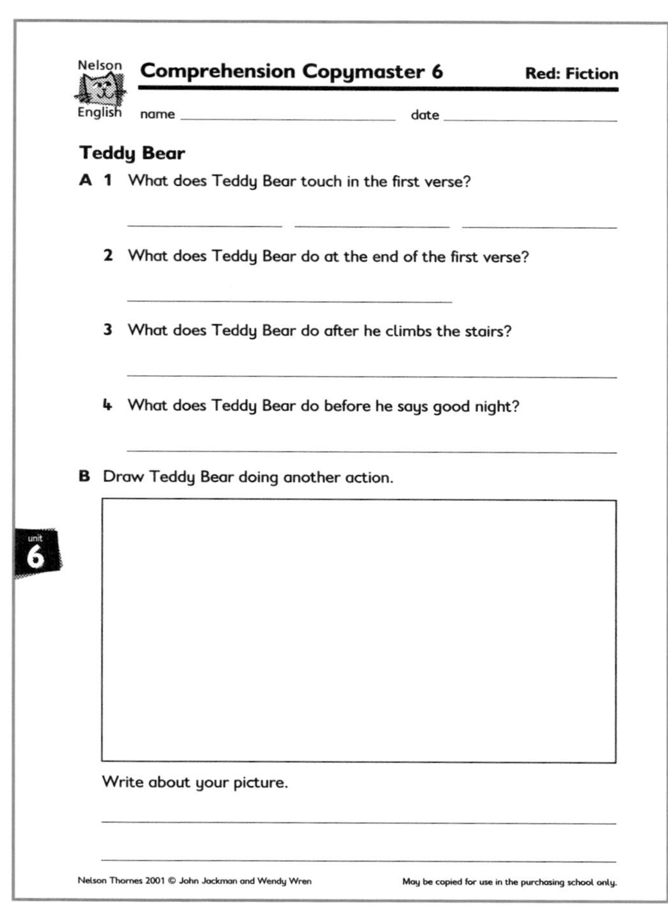

Nelson English

Comprehension Copymaster 6

Red: Fiction

name ______________ date ______________

Teddy Bear

A 1 What does Teddy Bear touch in the first verse?

__________ __________ __________

2 What does Teddy Bear do at the end of the first verse?

____

3 What does Teddy Bear do after he climbs the stairs?

____

4 What does Teddy Bear do before he says good night?

____

B Draw Teddy Bear doing another action.

Write about your picture.

____

____

unit 6

Nelson Thornes 2001 © John Jackman and Wendy Wren

May be copied for use in the purchasing school only.

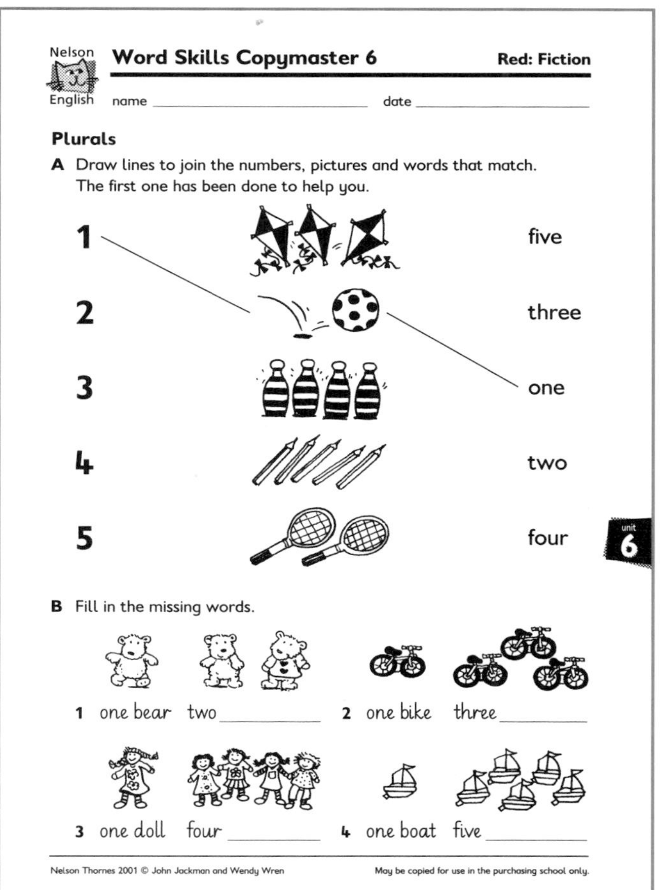

Nelson English

Word Skills Copymaster 6

Red: Fiction

name ______________ date ______________

Plurals

A Draw lines to join the numbers, pictures and words that match. The first one has been done to help you.

1 five

2 three

3 one

4 two

5 four

B Fill in the missing words.

1 one bear two __________ 2 one bike three __________

3 one doll four __________ 4 one boat five __________

unit 6

Nelson Thornes 2001 © John Jackman and Wendy Wren

May be copied for use in the purchasing school only.

Nelson English

Writing Copymaster 6

Red: Fiction

name ______________ date ______________

Teddy Bear

Teddy Bear,

Teddy Bear, wash your __________.

Teddy Bear,

Teddy Bear, tie your __________.

Teddy Bear,

Teddy Bear, __________ about.

Teddy Bear,

Teddy Bear, sing and __________.

unit 6

Nelson Thornes 2001 © John Jackman and Wendy Wren

May be copied for use in the purchasing school only.

unit 6

unit 6 Toys

Toys & In the Park

Non-fiction

National Literacy Strategy

Year 1 Term 2

Range

Non-fiction: simple dictionaries

Pupils should be taught:

Text level work

Reading comprehension

20 to use simple dictionaries, and to understand their alphabetical organisation;

Word level work

Phonological awareness, phonics and spelling

1 to secure identification, spelling and reading of initial . . . letter sounds in simple words;

3 • to discriminate, read and spell words with final consonant clusters . . .;

Word recognition, graphic knowledge and spelling

8 to investigate and learn spellings of words with 's' for plurals;

▲ to secure alphabetical ordering;

9 to read on sight . . . high frequency words identified for Year 1 . . . from Appendix List 1;

Sentence level work

Sentence construction and punctuation

5 to continue demarcating sentences in writing, ending a sentence with a full stop;

6 to use the term sentence appropriately to identify sentences in text, i.e. those demarcated by capital letters and full stops;

7 to use capital letters . . . for names and for the start of a sentence;

Text level work

Writing composition

▲ to make their own simple dictionary pages;

25 . . . to use simple sentences to describe, based on examples from reading; . . . and to organise in lists . . .

Teaching Notes

Poster: Shared reading

Text level work

Introduce the subject of toys and ask questions such as:

- What is your favourite toy?
- Which toy have you had the longest?
- What is the newest toy you have?

Display the poster and discuss with the children what they can see in the picture. Ask them to say what toys the children are playing with (i.e. skateboard, boat, ball, frisby, bat and ball, kite, roller skates, etc.); point to the words they use on the vocabulary strip. Can they spot the game the children are playing which requires no toy (hide and seek)? Do the children have a park near where they live? Do they play in the park? What sort of games do they play? Do they take toys to the park?

The first list on the vocabulary strip is the names of the main objects in the picture. Read through the object words with the children and ask if they notice anything about the list (i.e. it is in alphabetical order). The second list on the vocabulary strip deals with action words (see Word level work).

Suggest the names of other toys not pictured on the poster. Invite individuals to come forward and indicate where on the vocabulary list each word would go, depending on its initial letter. Avoid suggesting toys with the same initial letter as those already on the list as, at this stage, alphabetical ordering need only be by first letter.

Word level work

Refresh the children's memories about '-ng' words, which can be separated into two main categories: those in which '-ng' is a phoneme within the root word, e.g. *bang*, and those in which '-ng' is part of a suffix, e.g. *playing*. In both cases, help the children to hear the nasal 'ng' sound.

Given that 'ing' is used to form the present continuous tense (e.g. *He is playing.*), ask volunteers to suggest sentences about what is happening in the picture on the poster. When they refer to the actions listed in the vocabulary strip, point this out. Encourage the class to note that these words all end in 'ing'.

See whether anyone can suggest action words (verbs) other than those listed and, if so, make a list of these on the board. Ask the children to copy some of the 'ing' words, drawing a small picture next to each to indicate they are aware of its meaning.

Play a word game with different children miming an action at your suggestion (e.g. *digging, hopping, jumping, shouting*). The others guess what they are doing, giving their answers using an 'ing' word.

Use **Word Skills Copymaster 6 Non-fiction** for support with 'ing' words.

Sentence level work

Acting as scribe, ask the children to dictate a sentence about the poster. Write it without the initial capital letter and full stop. Invite suggestions about what mistakes you have made. If appropriate, invite a volunteer to correct your errors. Invite suggestions for another sentence. This time, write it correctly, and invite a child to circle the two things (capital letter and full stop) that show it is a sentence.

Pupil's book

Text level work

Introduction

Following on from the poster work, the pupil's book shows two pages of a simple picture dictionary which continues the theme of toys.

Discuss the pages with the children, leading them to understand that each dictionary entry has a word that is the name of a toy, an explanation of the word (definition), an illustration of the object, and that the words are arranged in alphabetical order.

Ask the children to suggest names of other toys. Make a list on the board and encourage them to say where on the dictionary pages each new word would go, e.g. *roller-skates* would go after *kite* and before *skipping-rope*. The children may suggest words with the same letters as words in the pupil's book. Explain alphabetical ordering by second and third letters, so the children realise there is a mechanism for doing so, even though this work is not tackled until later in the course.

Reading comprehension

In section A of **Comprehension Copymaster 6 Non-fiction** children are required to answer questions establishing literal comprehension of the passage in the pupil's book. Section B provides practice in alphabetical ordering. Section A can be approached as a class discussion, in guided or independently working groups, or individually.

Word level work

Important words

Use various alphabet charts, if available, to establish the concept of simple (first letter) alphabetical ordering. Discuss why ordering items in this way can be helpful, perhaps using simple reference books and dictionaries to demonstrate, emphasising that if things were arranged randomly in such books it would be much more difficult to find them.

Teach the children an alphabet song to help them to begin to remember the order of letters in the alphabet.

Remind the children that letters have names as well as sounds, and ensure everyone is familiar and confident in recognising both.

Ask individual children, pairs or groups to copy the letters of the alphabet down the left-hand side of a sheet of paper. Next to each letter, ask the children to write the name of an object (e.g. a toy) beginning with that letter. Spelling may cause some problems but, for the purpose of this activity, the most important aspect is that the initial letters are correct.

This activity can be repeated using different categories (e.g. household/classroom objects, foods, etc.) or practised verbally, in the form of the memory game 'I went to market and I bought . . .', with each child adding an item beginning with the next letter of the alphabet.

The high-frequency words for this unit, to be taught as 'sight recognition' words, are as follows.

boy
girl
house
home
little

Sentence level work

Sentences and capital letters

Having discussed toys and games, ask a child to say what is their favourite toy. Write on the board (for example): *The toy Alice likes best is her Barbie.* Point out that the initial letter of a person's name is always a capital (or upper case) letter. Ask each child to write a similar sentence about their neighbour's preference in toys or games.

Remind them that their sentence must begin with a capital (upper case) letter and finish with a full stop, and that names must also begin with capital (upper case) letters.

Text level work

Writing composition

Writing Copymaster 6 Non-fiction requires children to put into alphabetical order some simple sight vocabulary. The copymaster includes the alphabet, to provide support for children who are still unsure of alphabetical order. For children who can cope without having the alphabet written out for reference, cover or ink it out on the copymaster.

If possible, let the children work in pairs/groups and make their own simple picture dictionaries connected to topic work, e.g. animals. Explain that there will be three stages for each word:

1 write the word
2 draw a picture to illustrate the word
3 write an explanation (definition) of the word.

Use one sheet of paper for each word and give each group of children a different set of letters to work on, so that the finished class work can be displayed in alphabetical order, as a complete dictionary.

Copymaster answers

Comprehension Copymaster 6

A 1 doll
2 cuddly toy
3 kite
4 kite

B 1 'Crayons' would come after ball and before doll.
2 'Football' would come after doll and before kite.
3 'Yo-yo' would come after teddy bear.

Word Skills Copymaster 6

1 Simon is kicking the ball.
2 The dog is chasing the ball.
3 Indira is flying her new kite.
4 Lenny is throwing the frisbee.
5 Lara is riding her bike.
6 The baby is digging in the sand.

Writing Copymaster 6

and
boy
cat
for
go
he
is
look
mum
on
play
saw
tree
up
we
you

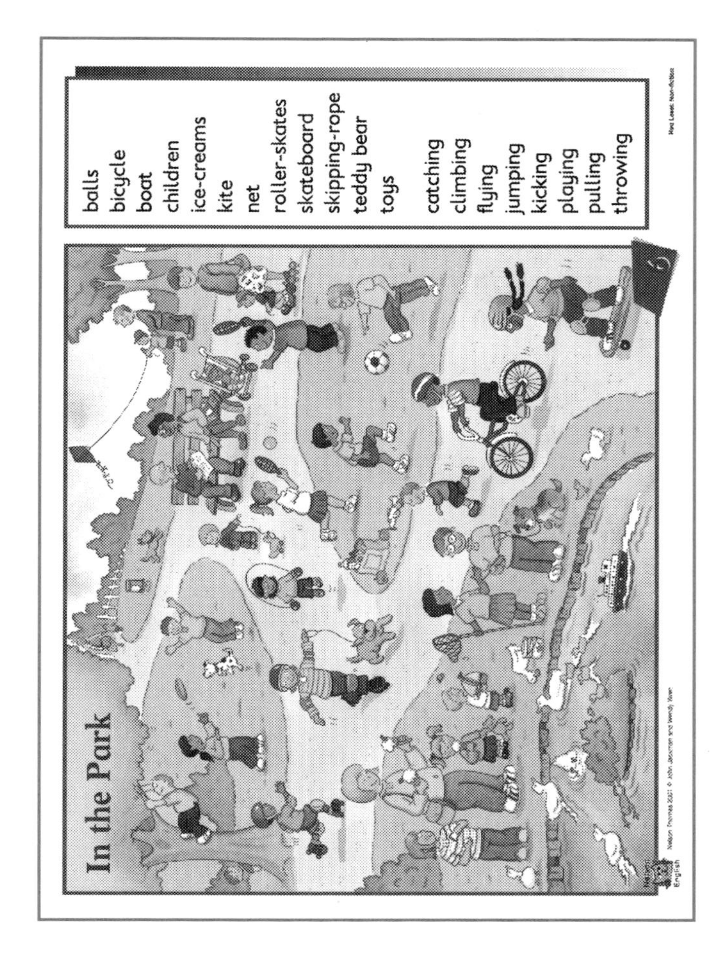

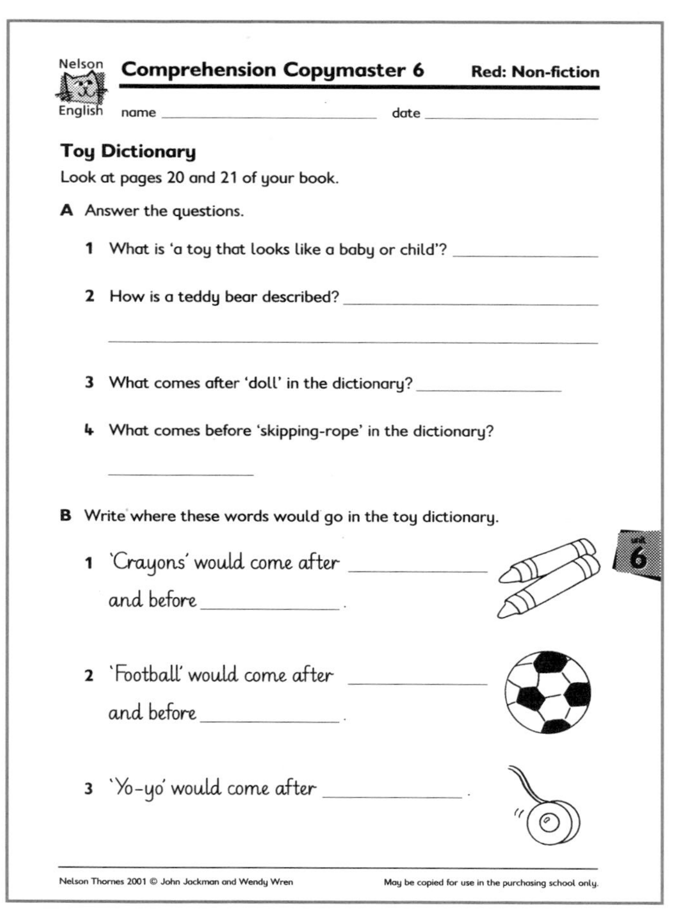
Nelson English

Comprehension Copymaster 6 **Red: Non-fiction**

name ______________ date ______________

Toy Dictionary

Look at pages 20 and 21 of your book.

A Answer the questions.

1 What is 'a toy that looks like a baby or child'? ______________

2 How is a teddy bear described? ______________

3 What comes after 'doll' in the dictionary? ______________

4 What comes before 'skipping-rope' in the dictionary? ______________

B Write where these words would go in the toy dictionary.

1 'Crayons' would come after ______________ and before ______________.

2 'Football' would come after ______________ and before ______________.

3 'Yo-yo' would come after ______________.

Nelson Thornes 2001 © John Jackman and Wendy Wren — May be copied for use in the purchasing school only.

Nelson English

Word Skills Copymaster 6 **Red: Non-fiction**

name ______________ date ______________

'ing' words

Choose an 'ing' word from the box to finish each sentence.

digging	flying	kicking
riding	throwing	chasing

1 Simon is ______________ the ball.

2 The dog is ______________ the ball.

3 Indira is ______________ her new kite.

4 Lenny is ______________ the frisbee.

5 Lara is ______________ her bike.

6 The baby is ______________ in the sand.

Nelson Thornes 2001 © John Jackman and Wendy Wren — May be copied for use in the purchasing school only.

Nelson English

Writing Copymaster 6 **Red: Non-fiction**

name ______________ date ______________

Alphabetical order

Write the words from the box in alphabetical order.

a b c d e f g h i j k l m n o p q r s t u v w x y z

boy	______
up	______
look	______
we	______
and	______
saw	______
on	______
for	______
he	______
is	______
tree	______
go	______
you	______
play	______
cat	______
mum	______

Nelson Thornes 2001 © John Jackman and Wendy Wren — May be copied for use in the purchasing school only.

unit 6

unit 7 Homes

Hansel and Gretel & A strange House

Fiction

National Literacy Strategy

Year 1 Term 3

Range

Fiction: stories about fantasy worlds

Pupils should be taught:

Text level work

Reading comprehension

5 to re-tell stories, to give the main points in sequence and to pick out significant incidents;

6 to prepare and re-tell stories orally, identifying and using some of the more formal features of story language;

8 to compare and contrast stories with a variety of settings . . .;

Word level work

Word recognition, graphic knowledge and spelling

4 to read on sight . . . high frequency words identified for Year 1 . . . from Appendix List 1;

Vocabulary extension

9 the terms 'vowel' and 'consonant';

Sentence level work

Grammatical awareness

4 about word order, e.g. by re-ordering sentences, ... and discussing the reasons why;

Sentence construction and punctuation

6 through reading and writing, to reinforce knowledge of term *sentence* from previous terms;

Text level work

Writing composition

14 to write stories using simple settings, e.g. based on previous reading.

Teaching Notes

Poster: Shared reading

Text level work

The text on the poster is the beginning of the story 'Hansel and Gretel'. Begin by asking if any of the children are familiar with the story. Some children will probably have heard the story, so encourage them to piece it together orally for the rest of the class. If there is disagreement about the details, use the opportunity to discuss different versions. Why do they think the details of the story may differ?

Read the extract to the children, pointing to the words as you read, and asking them to follow carefully.

Discuss the incidents in the story, asking the children to help you compile a list which reflects the narrative sequence (i.e. what happened and when).

- The reader is introduced to the main characters.
- The woodman and his wife talk about how poor they are and how they cannot feed the children.
- They decide to take the children into the wood and leave them.
- The next day the woodman and his wife take the children into the wood.
- They leave the children alone in the wood.

Base a class discussion on the following questions to encourage the children to think about the characters and their own response to the story.

- Why did the woodman and his wife decide to leave the children in the wood?
- What do you think about this?
- What would you have done if you were the woodman or his wife?
- How do you think the woodman and his wife felt when they left the children in the wood?

- How do you think Hansel and Gretel felt when their parents left them?

Word level work

Use an alphabet frieze or write on the board the 26 letters. Remind the children that each letter has both a sound and a name and that these are different. Invite volunteers to say the letter names from the alphabet, and then invite others to suggest the (short) sound of each letter.

Explain that there are five letters that are particularly important, and that nearly every word we write has at least one of these five letters. Write the letters *a, e, i, o, u* and explain that these are the five important 'vowel' letters. Copy onto the board the sentence from the poster *There was once a poor woodman and his wife.* Then select volunteers to come forward and point out, circle or underline the vowel letters in each word in turn.

Ask which two of the vowel letters can be short words in their own right (*a* and *I*). Use this early awareness to begin to establish that *I* must always be a capital when used as a word, whether or not it appears at the beginning of a sentence, whereas *a* follows the rules for any other word when it comes to capitalisation. Ask for suggestions of sentences in which *a* and *I* appear as words in their own right, and write these up. Capitalise as appropriate and draw the children's attention to the correct use of capital letters.

Having explored the five vowels, write on the board *consonant*. Tell the children that, of the 26 letters of the alphabet, five are vowels and the rest are consonants. Read through the letters on the alphabet frieze again, and ask the children to raise their hands (or stand) when a vowel is read out.

Sentence level work

Remind the children of the main features of a sentence, i.e. that it is a group of words that makes sense, begins with a capital letter and ends with a full stop. At this point, you may be asked about sentences ending with question marks or exclamation marks. Explain that each of these punctuation marks has a built-in full stop and can be used to end a sentence. It is not necessary to go into detail at this stage.

Write on the board *children. They two had* and ask a volunteer to read the words. Ask the children whether they form a sentence. If necessary, prompt by asking whether they make sense, as a sentence should. Agree that they don't but notice that the same words appear in a different order in a sentence on the poster – *They had two children.* From this, conclude that, whilst words have meaning, they need to be in the correct order to form proper sentences.

Write *all wood. Hansel dark, alone the Gretel in and were frightening* and invite the children to find the sentence on the poster which has the same words, but in the correct order (last sentence on poster).

Pupil's book

Text level work

Introduction

The extract in the pupil's book summarises the events covered on the poster and continues the story of Hansel and Gretel. It can be used as a whole-class/group text to investigate incidents and settings in stories.

If the poster has not been used, explain the beginning of the story, then read the text in the pupil's book, pointing to the words as you read, and encouraging the children to follow carefully.

After the first reading, encourage the children to tell you the story in their own words, prompting them by asking questions such as:

- What happened next?
- What did the children do then?

Base a class/group discussion on the following points to focus the children's attention on story setting:

Pages 24 and 25

Where does this part of the story take place?	(the wood)
What words are used to describe it?	(*big/dark/frightening*)
What other words could you use to describe it?	(e.g. *gloomy, spooky, scary*)
How would you feel if you were alone in the wood?	
How did Hansel and Gretel feel?	(frightened)

Page 26

What is different about this part of the wood?	(the hut)
What words are used to describe the hut?	(*little*; walls – *bread*; roof – *cake*; windows – *sweets*)
What other words could you use to describe it?	(e.g. *small, strange*)
How would you feel if you came across the hut?	

Page 27

How do you think Hansel and Gretel felt before the old woman appeared?

How do you think Hansel and Gretel felt after the old woman appeared?

What would you have done next if you were Hansel or Gretel?

Reading comprehension

Comprehension Copymaster 7 Fiction requires the children to pick out literal information from the pupil's book. Space is given for the children to write simple sentences in response to some questions, but one-word/phrase answers are acceptable.

The comprehension questions can be approached as a class discussion, in guided or independently working groups, or individually.

Word level work

Vowels and consonants

Remind the children of the work done with the poster on vowels and consonants. Ask them to copy the names of the two children in the story (*Hansel* and *Gretel*), and to neatly circle or underline the vowel letters in each word.

Next, ask the children to write their own names and, again, to highlight the vowel letters. Then ask them to write the letters in their own names in two lists, the vowels in the first list and the consonants in the second.

The high-frequency words for this unit, to be taught as 'sight recognition' words, are as follows.

can't
don't
good
from
as

Sentence level work

Sentences

Give the children jumbled sentences to write correctly. **Word Skills Copymaster 7 Fiction** provides practice in rearranging words into sentences. Try to ensure that, when focusing on word order, the children don't overlook the need for an initial capital letter and a closing full stop.

unit 7

Text level work

Writing composition

Following on from the poster and pupil's book discussion, the children should build up lists of words to describe given settings. This can be done in the following ways.

- Providing pictures from magazines or travel brochures, showing a variety of scenes. Choose images without human figures, so the children are not tempted to write about the people and what they are doing rather than concentrating on choosing words to describe the setting.
- Using photographs which you or the children can bring in of places you/they have visited.
- Using **Writing Copymaster 7 Fiction**, which provides pictures of three settings for the children to caption with descriptive words. The children could be asked to colour the pictures and add further descriptive words/phrases as a result.

Copymaster answers

Comprehension Copymaster 7

Some children may write sentences, others just words or phrases.

1 big, dark
2 frightened
3 find their way home
4 a little hut
5 the walls
6 the roof
7 the wall
8 the window
9 an old woman

Word Skills Copymaster 7

1 I don't like this wood.
2 There is a little hut.
3 The roof is made of cake.
4 The windows are made of sweets.

Writing Copymaster 7

Individual answers.

Hansel and Gretel

There was once a poor woodman and his wife. They had two children. The boy was called Hansel and the girl was called Gretel. The woodman and his wife were so poor they had no money for food.

One night when the children were asleep, the woodman and his wife sat talking.

"We are so poor," said the wife.

"We cannot feed the children," said the woodman.

"We must take them into the wood and leave them there," said the wife.

"Yes," said the woodman. "Someone may find them and look after them."

The next day, the woodman and his wife took the children into the wood and left them there. Hansel and Gretel were all alone in the dark, frightening wood.

Red Level: Fiction

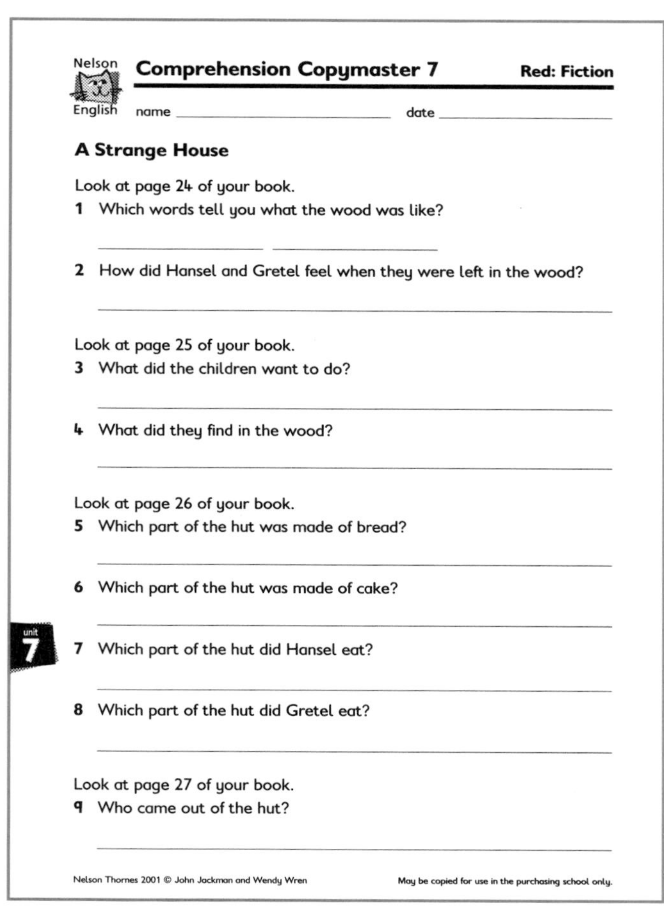

Nelson English **Comprehension Copymaster 7** **Red: Fiction**

name ______________ date ______________

A Strange House

Look at page 24 of your book.

1 Which words tell you what the wood was like?

2 How did Hansel and Gretel feel when they were left in the wood?

Look at page 25 of your book.

3 What did the children want to do?

4 What did they find in the wood?

Look at page 26 of your book.

5 Which part of the hut was made of bread?

6 Which part of the hut was made of cake?

7 Which part of the hut did Hansel eat?

8 Which part of the hut did Gretel eat?

Look at page 27 of your book.

9 Who came out of the hut?

Nelson Thornes 2001 © John Jackman and Wendy Wren

May be copied for use in the purchasing school only.

unit 7

Nelson English **Word Skills Copymaster 7** **Red: Fiction**

name ______________ date ______________

Sentences

Put the words in the right order to show what the children said.

1 like this wood. I don't

2 is little hut. There a

3 made is of roof cake. The

4 are of made The windows sweets.

Nelson Thornes 2001 © John Jackman and Wendy Wren

May be copied for use in the purchasing school only.

unit 7

Nelson English **Writing Copymaster 7** **Red: Fiction**

name ______________ date ______________

Describing Places

Write some words to describe each place.

Nelson Thornes 2001 © John Jackman and Wendy Wren

May be copied for use in the purchasing school only.

unit 7

Homes

unit 7

Inside a House

Non-fiction

National Literacy Strategy

Year 1 Term 3

Range

Non-fiction: information texts including recounts of observations, visits, events

Pupils should be taught:

Text level work

Reading comprehension

19 to identify simple questions and use text to find answers. To locate parts of text that give particular information including labelled diagrams and charts . . .;

Word level work

Phonological awareness, phonics and spelling

1 the common spelling patterns for each of the long vowel phonemes: *ee*, *ai*, *ie*, *oa*, *oo* (long as in *moon*)
Appendix List 3:
- to identify phonemes in speech and writing;
- to segment words into phonemes for spelling;

Word recognition, graphic knowledge and spelling

4 to read on sight . . . high frequency words identified for Year 1 . . . from Appendix List 1;

Vocabulary extension

9 the terms *'vowel'* and *'consonant'*;

Sentence level work

Grammatical awareness

4 about word order, e.g. by re-ordering sentences, predicting words from previous text, grouping a range of words that might 'fit', and discussing the reasons why;

Sentence construction and punctuation

6 through reading and writing, to reinforce knowledge of the term *sentence* from previous terms;

Text level work

Writing composition

21 to use the language and features of non-fiction texts, e.g. labelled diagrams, caption for pictures, to make class books . . .

Teaching Notes

Poster: Shared reading

Text level work

Explain to the children that you are going to do some work on homes. Ask them how they could let you know what their home looks like, e.g. talk about it, write about it, draw it, bring in a photograph, etc. Depending on the home circumstances of the children in the class, you may choose to modify or avoid specific reference to the pupils' own home environment.

Display the poster. Ask the children what they can see in the picture. As they identify the objects ask them to find the corresponding word in the vocabulary strip. The vocabulary strip is in alphabetical order and can be used to reinforce the work on alphabetical order from Unit 6 Non-fiction.

Ask the children how they would describe the house e.g. big, small, cosy, colourful, cluttered, roomy, etc. Ask further questions to prompt discussion, e.g.:
- Would you like to live in this house?
- Why?/Why not?
- How is this house similar/different to your home?

Word level work

Revisit earlier work in the parallel Fiction unit (Hansel and Gretel) about the five vowel letters and why they are particularly important. Remind the children that nearly every word we write has at least one of these five letters. Invite one of the children to suggest a short sentence about the poster for you to write on the board. Invite volunteers to come forward to identify the vowel letters in each word.

Write on the board the following words: *my, by, try, fly, cry, sly*. Again, invite the children to identify the vowels. They will tell you that there are none. Explain that, in a few special words, 'y' stands in place of the vowel letter 'i'. Can the children think of any other words like this (e.g. *pry, dry, fry, ply, wry, spy, sty, sky*, etc.)? As an extension, some children might be invited to learn the spelling of some of these special words.

Having revisited the five vowels and 'y', recap on the concept of consonants. Using an alphabet frieze, and ask the children to raise their hands (or stand) when a vowel is read out and remain seated for the consonants, or vice versa.

Recap on the distinction between the name of a letter and its sound, then focus on the sounds made by the vowel letters. Whilst there is no easy way to teach the range of letters that can represent the 'long' sound of the five vowel letters (their grapheme/phoneme relationships), many children find it helpful to begin by learning about the modifier (or 'magic') 'e'.

Write on the board the word *home*. Sound the letters individually with the children, and discover that the 'short' sounds of each letter, when sounded together, don't 'say' *home*. Explain that the vowel letter in a word usually 'says its own name' when an 'e' is added to the end of the word. A particularly useful way of introducing this concept is to use clusters of letters that are words in their own right without the modifier 'e', such as *not* and (*note*). Other examples include:

can	cap	mad	man	mat	tap	van
	plan	slat				
fin	hid	kit	pin	pip	rid	rip
	win					
slid	strip					
cod	hop	not	pop	rob	rod	wok
cut	hug	tub				
plum						

There are no words that the children are likely to come across in which the modifier 'e' relates to a short vowel 'e', i.e. no words such as *met, get, led* can take a magic 'e' to form another word. This point becomes more significant later when seeking to help the children decide the most reasonable and likely spelling for a word which incorporates the 'ee' phoneme (i.e. *peel* not *pele*).

Sentence level work

Remind the children about the main features of a sentence. Write on the board a simple sentence, such as *There is one bedroom in this house*. Remind the children about the initial capital letter, and the need to end with a full stop. (As noted previously, in *Nelson English* we teach that the punctuation marks ? or ! have a built-in full stop and so can be used to end sentences, but there is no need to mention this at this stage unless a child raises the issue with you.)

Write the following three jumbled sentences on the board:
a yellow There is rug the in bathroom. (*There is a yellow rug in the bathroom.*)
kitchen. in kettle the The is (*The kettle is in the kitchen.*)
is sitting The dog in front of fire. the (*The dog is sitting in front of the fire.*).
Ask a volunteer to read the first set of the words. Ask whether they are a sentence. Ask the children to rearrange the words to form a sentence. Act as scribe as the children offer a final sentence, or ask a volunteer to write the final sentence, reminding him/her about the need for an initial capital letter, a final full stop and word order that makes sense. Repeat with the other two jumbled sentences. This activity can be repeated with jumbled sentences suggested by the children.

Pupil's book

Text level work

Introduction

Following on from the poster work, the pupil's book shows the same house with added labels, making it an annotated diagram.

Discuss the picture with the children, leading them to understand that this is another way of presenting information, i.e. a diagram with labels.

Reading comprehension

Comprehension Copymaster 7 Non-fiction requires the children to look closely at the labelled diagram of the house and find literal information for questions 1 to 7, find inferential information for question 8 and to express a personal preference and give reasons for question 9.

The comprehension questions can be approached as a class discussion, through guided or independently working groups, or individually.

Word level work

Magic 'e' words

Reintroduce magic 'e' words with the names of items illustrated in the pupil's book (e.g. *tile, bone, game, fire, cake, plate*). **Word Skills Copymaster 7 Non-fiction** provides practice with modifier, or magic 'e', words.

The following words, many of which are associated with homes and houses, can be used to further explore the concept of modifier, or magic 'e', words. (**Bold** type denotes words that are words in their own right both with and without the magic 'e'.)

bake	cake	make	shake	game	name	flame
lane	plate	save	spade	**tape**	wave	shave
shade	shape					

bike like **bite** **kite** **site** drive pile
tile smile **pine** **wine** **shine** **hide** side
wide **slide** wife **pipe** wipe **fire**

bone **cone** stone rope **slope** hole pole
home joke poke woke broke smoke hose
rose close

use fuse **cube** **tube** blue glue

According to ability, children might be given two or three words and asked to illustrate them and/or write a sentence including one or more of the words. Also, a cluster of words from the same basic spelling family (e.g. 'o-e' words, such as *bone*) could be set for the children to learn.

The high-frequency words for this unit, to be taught as 'sight recognition' words, are as follows.

our
your
back
help
will

Sentence level work

Sentences

Offer the children one or two short sentences about the picture in the pupil's book, omitting the capital letters and full stops. Ask them to spot the deliberate mistakes and write the sentences correctly.

Text level work

Writing composition

Modelling their work on the illustration in the pupil's book, the children should attempt to make an annotated diagram of one of the following:

- their home
- one room in their home
- a room they would like to have
- the classroom.

For children who would find the above task too difficult, **Writing Copymaster 7 Non-fiction** provides a simple drawing of a room with a word box to help the children write labels.

Copymaster answers

Comprehension Copymaster 7

1 four (*some children may also count the hall and landing.*)
2 living room
3 bedroom
4 window
5 door
6 lamp
7 shelf/stairs/sink
8 There is a cot in the bedroom.
9 *Individual answers.*

Word Skills Copymaster 7

A 1 tape
2 cape
3 pipe
4 pine
5 tube
6 slope

B 1 cake
2 nose
3 bone
4 bike

Writing Copymaster 7

Children should correctly label the diagram.

Inside a House

bath
bathroom
bed
bedroom
chair
cot
door
hall
house
kitchen
landing
living-room
mat
rug
sink
sofa
stairs
table
toilet
wardrobe
window

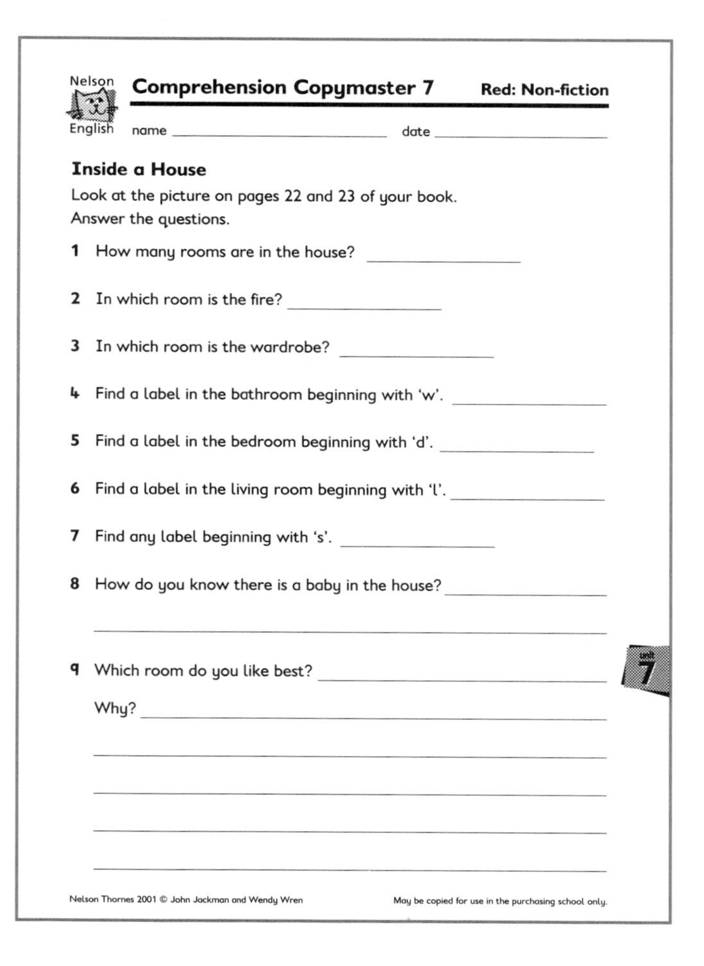

Nelson English

Comprehension Copymaster 7 — Red: Non-fiction

name ________ date ________

Inside a House

Look at the picture on pages 22 and 23 of your book.
Answer the questions.

1 How many rooms are in the house? ________

2 In which room is the fire? ________

3 In which room is the wardrobe? ________

4 Find a label in the bathroom beginning with 'w'. ________

5 Find a label in the bedroom beginning with 'd'. ________

6 Find a label in the living room beginning with 'l'. ________

7 Find any label beginning with 's'. ________

8 How do you know there is a baby in the house? ________

9 Which room do you like best? ________

Why? ________

Nelson Thornes 2001 © John Jackman and Wendy Wren — May be copied for use in the purchasing school only.

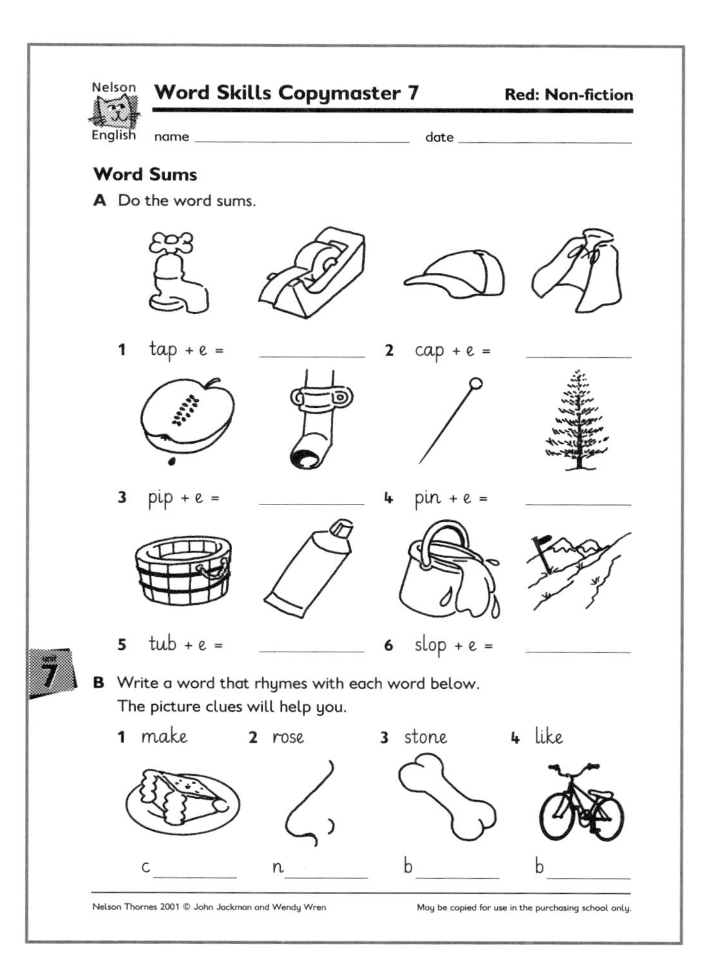

Nelson English

Word Skills Copymaster 7 — Red: Non-fiction

name ________ date ________

Word Sums

A Do the word sums.

1 tap + e = ________ 2 cap + e = ________

3 pip + e = ________ 4 pin + e = ________

5 tub + e = ________ 6 slop + e = ________

B Write a word that rhymes with each word below.
The picture clues will help you.

1 make 2 rose 3 stone 4 like

c________ n________ b________ b________

Nelson Thornes 2001 © John Jackman and Wendy Wren — May be copied for use in the purchasing school only.

Nelson English

Writing Copymaster 7 — Red: Non-fiction

name ________ date ________

A Room

Write the words from the box as labels on the picture.

bed chair rug wardrobe desk shelf

Nelson Thornes 2001 © John Jackman and Wendy Wren — May be copied for use in the purchasing school only.

Tigers unit 8

Mr Tig the Tiger

Fiction

National Literacy Strategy

Year 1 Term 3

Range

Fiction: stories about fantasy worlds

Pupils should be taught:

Text level work

Reading comprehension

5 to re-tell stories, to give the main points in sequence and to pick out significant incidents;
6 to prepare and re-tell stories orally, identifying and using some of the more formal features of story language;
8 to compare and contrast stories with a variety of settings . . .;

Word level work

Word recognition, graphic knowledge and spelling

6 to investigate and learn spelling of verbs with 'ed' (past tense), 'ing' (present tense) endings;
9 to read on sight . . . high frequency words identified for Year 1 . . . from Appendix List 1;

Sentence level work

Sentence construction and punctuation

5 other common uses of capitalisation, e.g. for personal titles (*Mr*, *Miss*), headings, book titles, emphasis;
7 to add question marks to questions;

Text level work

Writing composition

13 to write about significant incidents from known stories.

Teaching Notes

Poster: Shared reading

Text level work

The poster shows the beginning of a story called 'Mr Tig the Tiger'. Relatively few stories for this age group are set in a fantasy world (i.e. if 'fantasy world' refers to somewhere other than this world.) The 'real' world setting of this story becomes fantastical because of the tiger toy that can talk.

Read the poster to the children, pointing to the words as you read, and asking them to follow carefully.

Discuss the incidents in the story, asking the children to help you compile a list which reflects the narrative sequence:

- Bimla had to tidy her messy bedroom.
- Her cousin Satia was coming to stay.
- Dad wanted the room tidied.
- Bimla could not go out to play until it was done.
- Bimla began to tidy the books.
- Dad came in with a bin bag.
- He was pleased Bimla had begun to tidy up.
- Bimla wanted to know what the bag was for.
- Dad told her she should throw away some of the old things.

Base a class discussion on the following points to encourage the children to think about their response to the story and the characters.

- Why was Dad cross?
- Do you think Bimla wanted to tidy up or go out to play?
- How do you think Bimla felt about having to tidy up?
- How do you think she felt when Dad said she could throw away some of the old things?
- How would you feel?

Discuss the setting of the story. It is the familiar, everyday setting of a home and one to which many children will be able to relate. Contrast the setting with that on the Unit 7 Fiction poster. The setting and events of the story are 'realistic' up to this point (which makes for a contrast when, later in the story, the tiger speaks).

Word level work

Acting as scribe, ask the children to tell you what is happening in the picture. The objective is to encourage them to offer short sentences or phrases that contain a (continuous) present-tense verb with the 'ing' suffix, e.g. *Dad is pointing.*

Discuss how 'ing' is often added to an action word (verb) to tell us that the action is happening now. Encourage children to look around the room and suggest sentences using other action words that end in 'ing' about actions/situations happening 'now', for example *Our teacher is talking. We are listening. I am sitting on a chair.*

Sentence level work

Revise with the children the essential components of a sentence – that it should make sense, begin with a capital letter and end with a full stop. Invite a volunteer to suggest a sentence which relates to the picture on the poster. Write the suggestion on the board, and discuss whether and why it can be described as a sentence.

Write on the board a question that relates to the picture, e.g. *What is Bimla doing?* Ask whether this is a sentence. Check off each of the sentence criteria. When you come to the need for a full stop, ask whether this sentence has one. Some/most will say that it doesn't. Ask the class to look very closely at the question mark and notice that it has a full stop 'built into' it. Explain that questions are 'asking sentences' and should conform to the 'rules' of sentences by making sense, starting with a capital letter and ending with a punctuation mark that includes a full stop.

Ask the children to suggest other questions that might be asked about the illustration on the poster and write the suggestions on the board. When you have collected three or four questions, ask selected children in turn to come forward and circle one of the question marks. Ask others to come out and try to draw a question mark on the board.

Pupil's book

Text level work

Introduction

The pupil's book repeats and continues the beginning of the story of 'Mr Tig the Tiger' from the poster. It can be used as a whole-class/group text to investigate incidents and settings in stories.

Ask the children to follow carefully as you read the passage, pointing to the words as you read. After the first reading, encourage the children to tell you the story in their own words, prompting them by asking questions such as:

- What happened next?
- What did Bimla put in the bag first?

Move on to discuss the children's response to the story:

- Did you like it?
- What was your favourite part?
- What did you think about Bimla's dad making her tidy the room?
- What did you think when the tiger spoke?

At the end of the extract, the tiger says he can do lots of other things as well as talk. Discuss the children's ideas about what else Mr Tig can do. Encourage the children to discuss what they think might happen next in the story. Will Bimla tell her dad or her cousin Satia? Will Bimla and Mr Tig have adventures together?

Reading comprehension

Comprehension Copymaster 8 Fiction contains multiple-choice style questions and requires the children to pick out literal information from the pupil's book and choose the correct ending to each statement.

The comprehension questions can be approached as a class discussion, in guided or independently working groups, or individually.

Word level work

'ing' and 'ed' words

Read through the passage with the group, stopping each time you come across a word with the 'ing' suffix. Remind the children that these are action words describing what is happening now (i.e. present tense). Ask the children to copy some/all of the words and to add some of their own. At this stage, try to focus on verbs that take a simple 'ing' suffix without requiring either doubling or dropping of the final letter (e.g. *jump/jumped, open/opened* rather than *come/coming*). If the issue arises, explain that some other kinds of words end in 'ing', e.g. *everything, stuffing* but that these are not the same as action words.

Word Skills Copymaster 8 Fiction provides further practice with 'ing' action words.

Look through the passage in the pupil's book again and find the verbs that end in 'ed' (e.g.. *jumped* and *opened* on page 31). Ask the children to suggest other 'ed' verbs, then ask volunteers to put each word into a sentence. Help the children to realise that 'ed' verbs tell us about events that have happened in the past (i.e. past tense).

Write on the board some simple 'ed' verbs and ask the children to copy them, then to write a sentence using one of these action words.

The high-frequency words for this unit, to be taught as 'sight recognition' words, are as follows.

four
five
six
seven
blue

Sentence level work

Questions

Ask the children to practise writing question marks, drawing attention to the full stop at the foot of each.

Ask the children to find and copy a question from the passage in the pupil's book.

As an extension, ask the children to suggest words that are frequently used at the beginning of questions (e.g. *which, when, what, where, why, how*). List them on the board and encourage the children to notice that most begin with 'wh'.

The children already know that capital letters are used to begin sentences and also for proper nouns (notably names). Now draw attention to the fact that titles (e.g. *Mr, Mrs, Ms, Miss*) also commence with a capital letter. Ask the children to find and copy an example in the text (i.e. *Mr Tig*). If appropriate, extend this by writing the 'formal' names of known adults, such as teachers or family members. If the issue arises, explain that some people have other titles, such as *Doctor, Professor, Sir, Lady, Reverend, Rabbi,* rather than the more common titles, and that these, too, begin with a capital letter.

Text level work

Writing composition

Following on from the poster/pupil's book discussion, encourage the children to pick out an incident in the story that they liked, and to draw and write about it. The writing will vary from words and phrases to complete sentences, depending on individual ability.

For support, **Writing Copymaster 8 Fiction** consists of a drawing of Mr Tig. They can colour the picture and then write words/phrases/sentences to explain what other things they think Mr Tig can do.

Copymaster answers

Comprehension Copymaster 8

1 pleased
2 ripped
3 it had pieces missing
4 an ear missing
5 in the bag

Word Skills Copymaster 8

Pupils should correctly label the illustration.

Writing Copymaster 8

Individual answers.

Mr Tig the Tiger

Bimla had to tidy her room because her cousin, Satia, was coming to stay for the weekend.

Dad was cross that the room was in such a mess. Bimla could not go out to play until all the toys were put away and everything was neat and tidy.

She began to pick up the books and put them on the shelf. Dad came into the room carrying a black bin bag.

"Good girl," he said. "It won't take you very long."

"What's the bin bag for?" asked Bimla.

"I thought you could throw away some of the very old things."

"Why?" asked Bimla.

"Well," said Dad, "you have too much stuff in here and some of it is very old."

Nelson English

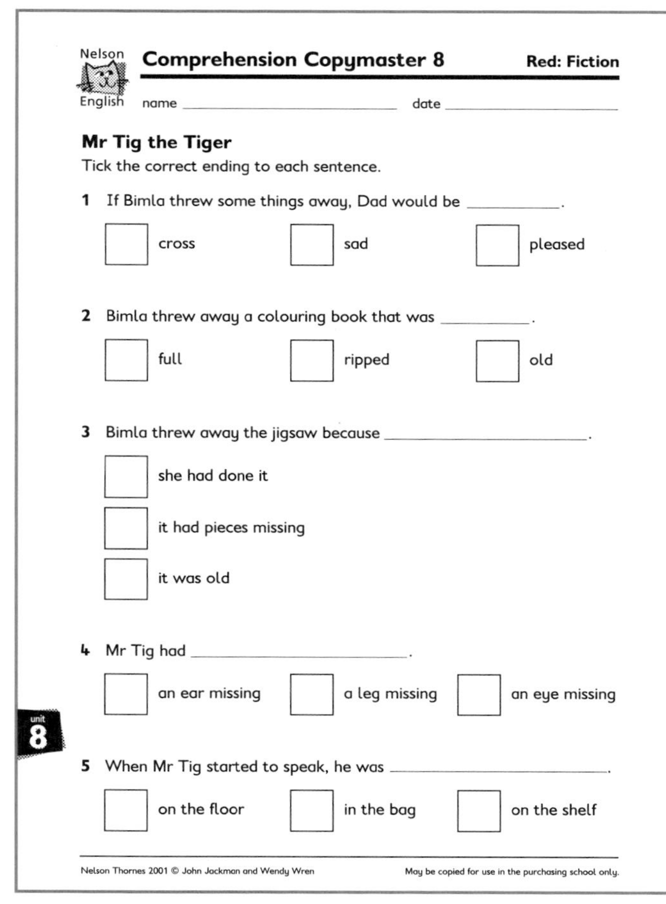

Nelson English

Comprehension Copymaster 8 — Red: Fiction

name ______________________ date ______________________

Mr Tig the Tiger

Tick the correct ending to each sentence.

1 If Bimla threw some things away, Dad would be __________.

☐ cross ☐ sad ☐ pleased

2 Bimla threw away a colouring book that was __________.

☐ full ☐ ripped ☐ old

3 Bimla threw away the jigsaw because __________.

☐ she had done it

☐ it had pieces missing

☐ it was old

4 Mr Tig had __________.

☐ an ear missing ☐ a leg missing ☐ an eye missing

5 When Mr Tig started to speak, he was __________.

☐ on the floor ☐ in the bag ☐ on the shelf

unit 8

Nelson Thornes 2001 © John Jackman and Wendy Wren — May be copied for use in the purchasing school only.

Nelson English

Word Skills Copymaster 8 — Red: Fiction

name ______________________ date ______________________

'ing' Words

Write the words from the box in the correct spaces on the picture.

playing, sleeping, eating, reading, holding, watching

unit 8

Nelson Thornes 2001 © John Jackman and Wendy Wren — May be copied for use in the purchasing school only.

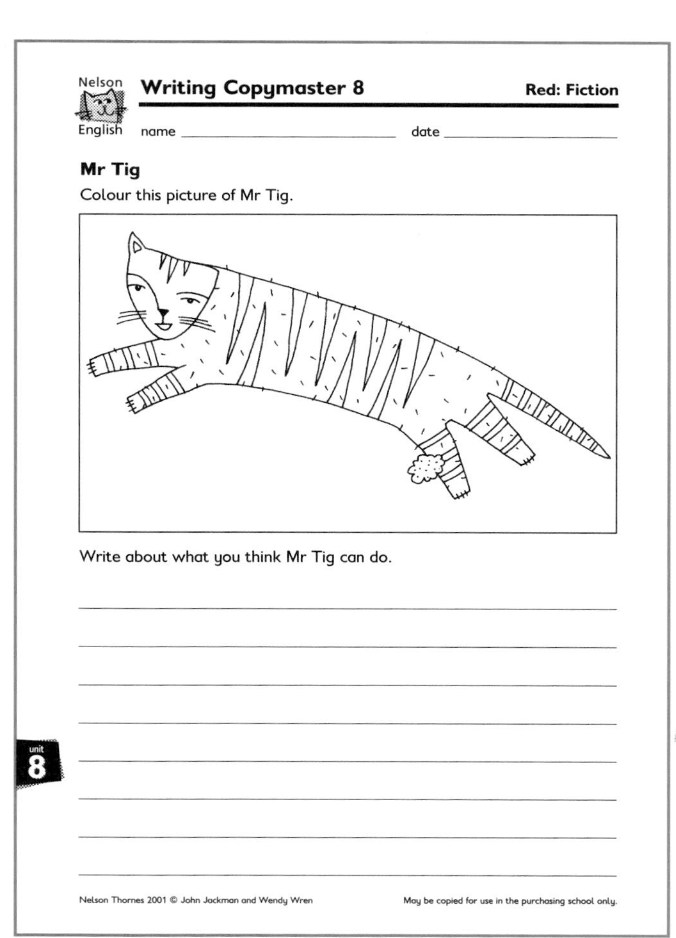

Nelson English

Writing Copymaster 8 — Red: Fiction

name ______________________ date ______________________

Mr Tig

Colour this picture of Mr Tig.

Write about what you think Mr Tig can do.

unit 8

Nelson Thornes 2001 © John Jackman and Wendy Wren — May be copied for use in the purchasing school only.

unit 8

Tigers unit 8

Tigers

Non-fiction

National Literacy Strategy

Year 1 Term 3

Range

Non-fiction: information texts including recounts of observations, visits, events

Pupils should be taught:

Text level work

Reading comprehension

17 to recognise that non-fiction books on similar themes can give different information and present similar information in different ways;

Word level work

Phonological awareness, phonics and spelling

1 the common spelling patterns for each of the long vowel phonemes: *ee . . . oo* (long as in *moon*)
Appendix List 3:
- to identify phonemes in speech and writing; . . .
- to segment words into phonemes for spelling;

Word recognition, graphic knowledge and spelling

4 to read on sight . . . high frequency words identified for Year 1 . . . from Appendix List 1;

Vocabulary extension

9 the terms *'vowel'* and *'consonant'*;

Sentence level work

Grammatical awareness

4 about word order, e.g. by re-ordering sentences, predicting words from previous text, grouping a range of words that might 'fit', and discussing the reasons why;

6 through reading and writing, to reinforce knowledge of the term *sentence* from previous terms;

Text level work

Writing composition

22 to write own questions prior to reading for information and to record answers, e.g. as lists, a completed chart, extended captions for display, a fact file on IT.

Teaching Notes

Poster: Shared reading

Text level work

Revise the work from Unit 5 Non-fiction on the difference between fiction and non-fiction. Remind the children that a non-fiction book gives us information.

Display the poster and discuss with the children what it shows, pointing out words they use on the vocabulary strip.

Through discussion, establish what the children know about tigers. What do they think about tigers? What would they like to find out about tigers?

Draw on the board a table with the following headings: *What we know about tigers, What we think about tigers, What we would like to know about tigers.* List the children's responses.

Ask the children to suggest captions for the pictures on the poster.

Word level work

Remind the children what they have learnt about vowels and consonants, and the difference between the name of a letter and its sound. Recap on modifier (or 'magic') 'e', which makes the vowel letter in a word 'say its own name' (e.g. *spin/spine*).

Write on the board the letter 'e'. Ask the children to offer the sound of the letter and then its name (or 'long' sound). Next write on the board the words *meat* and *feet* and ask the children to say the words aloud with you. Underline, or write in a different colour, the vowel digraph ('ea', 'ee'). Ask a volunteer to tell the class what sound is made by the two letters in each case. Once it is recognised that both make the long 'e' sound, write three or four other words, each of which includes either the 'ea' or 'ee' digraph, for example:

bee fee see
eel feel heel peel reel
deed feed need seed weed
been keen seen
deep jeep keep peep seep weep
feet meet
leek meek week

pea sea tea
beat eat heat meat neat peat teat
bean jeans lean mean
beam seam team
deal heal meal peal sea steal veal
beak leak speak teak weak
bead lead read
heap leap reap
beast east feast least yeast

For a more complete list, refer to the *Nelson Spelling* Teacher's Book.

Write on the board: *Tigers eat lots of food.* Tell the children that both the long 'e' sound and the long 'u' sound (even though there is no letter 'u') are to be found in the sentence. Ask who can guess which letter combinations make each of these vowel sounds (i.e. 'ea' and 'oo').

Only you will know the pace at which this type of work can be developed with a particular group or class but, if appropriate, ask the children to copy and then find all the letters making long 'u' sounds in the sentence *In June, tigers chew their food in the blue moonlight.*

Below is a selection of words with vowel digraphs for the long 'u' sound.

woo zoo
boom doom room
boot coot loot hoot root toot shoot
food mood
fool pool tool
hoof roof
hoop loop
moon noon soon spoon

dune June prune tune
lute cute use fuse rude nude cube
tube

blue clue glue true

chew dew few new stew yew
blew crew drew flew grew
screw threw

Again, for a more complete list, refer to the *Nelson Spelling* Teacher's Book.

As in the earlier units and, again, according to ability, two or three words might be selected from the list, and the children asked to illustrate them and/or write a sentence including one or more of the words. Also, a cluster of words from the same basic spelling family could be set for the children to learn.

Sentence level work

Once the children have offered captions for the pictures on the poster, write on the board some other possible openings for sentences about the pictures. Ask the children to study the pictures and vocabulary strip carefully and offer possible words/phrases to complete the sentences, e.g. *Tigers' coats are* _______ *and* _______.

This activity can be extended by writing on the board cloze sentences that relate to the pictures but do not specifically seek words available in the vocabulary strip. Invite the children to suggest a range of possible words that could be used to fill the gaps, e.g. *The tigers* ______ *through the* ______ *grass.* (e.g. *ran, walked, prowled, crept; brown, dry, tall, thick*).

Pupil's book

Text level work

Introduction

Following on from the poster work, the pupil's book shows more written and pictorial information about tigers.

Discuss the pages with the children, leading them to understand the different ways of presenting information, e.g. photographs, fact file. Have on hand some other reference books on tigers or big cats and let the children investigate other ways in which information can be presented, e.g. diagrams, captions, lists, etc.

Reading comprehension

Comprehension Copymaster 8 Non-fiction requires the children to find literal information from the captioned photographs and the fact file in the pupil's book. Section A is a simple cloze activity, and Section B required word/phrase answers. The comprehension questions can be approached as a class discussion, through guided or independently working groups, or individually.

Word level work

'oo' and 'ee'/'ea' vowel digraphs

Use **Word Skills Copymaster 8 Non-fiction** to continue work from the poster on the 'oo' vowel digraph.

Write the following 'ee' words on the board.

bee reel greed tree eel heel need
free deep weed jeep feed keep weep
seed see feel steep peel heed deed

The words can then be sorted according to their 'rime' patterns. Divide the rest of the board into four columns under the headings: *'ee' words, 'eel' words, 'eed' words, 'eep' words*. Invite children to sort the words under the correct headings, either by copying the headings and writing each word under the correct heading, or by coming forward and writing one word at a time under the correct heading on the board.

The high-frequency words for this unit, to be taught as 'sight recognition' words, are as follows.

eight
nine
ten
yellow
black

Sentence level work

Completing sentences

Similar activities to those undertaken with the poster can be developed with the pupil's book material, possibly by writing two or three sentences on the board, leaving a few gaps for the children to consider and inviting volunteers to come forward and write in their chosen words. Explore sentences in which more than one word will fit, and note the resulting variations in meaning.

Text level work

Writing composition

Writing Copymaster 8 Non-fiction has an illustration of a lion as a stimulus for the children to write questions focusing on what they would like to know about lions. The categories in the tiger Fact File can be used as a model for their questions, e.g.:

- What colour are lions?
- Is the male lion bigger or smaller than the female?
- What do lions eat?, etc.

Children are usually comfortable asking questions verbally but are likely to need help in writing them down. This work can be done individually or in groups. On a large sheet of paper, under the heading *What we want to find out about lions*, a group/class list of the children's questions could be compiled.

When the questions have been written, allow access to suitable, simple reference books in which the children can find the answers to their questions. On a large sheet of paper, under the heading *What we found out about lions*, the results of the children's research can be written.

Copymaster answers

Comprehension Copymaster 8

A 1 Tigers are big cats.
2 Siberia is a cold place.
3 India is a hot place.
4 A tigress can have as many as seven cubs.
5 The cubs feed from their mother's milk for eight weeks.

B 1 orange and black
2 at night
3 deer *or* wild pig
4 no

Word Skills Copymaster 8

1 orange
2 moon
3 food
4 boot
5 broom
6 hoof
7 tool
8 roots
9 pool
10 roof

Writing Copymaster 8

Individual answers

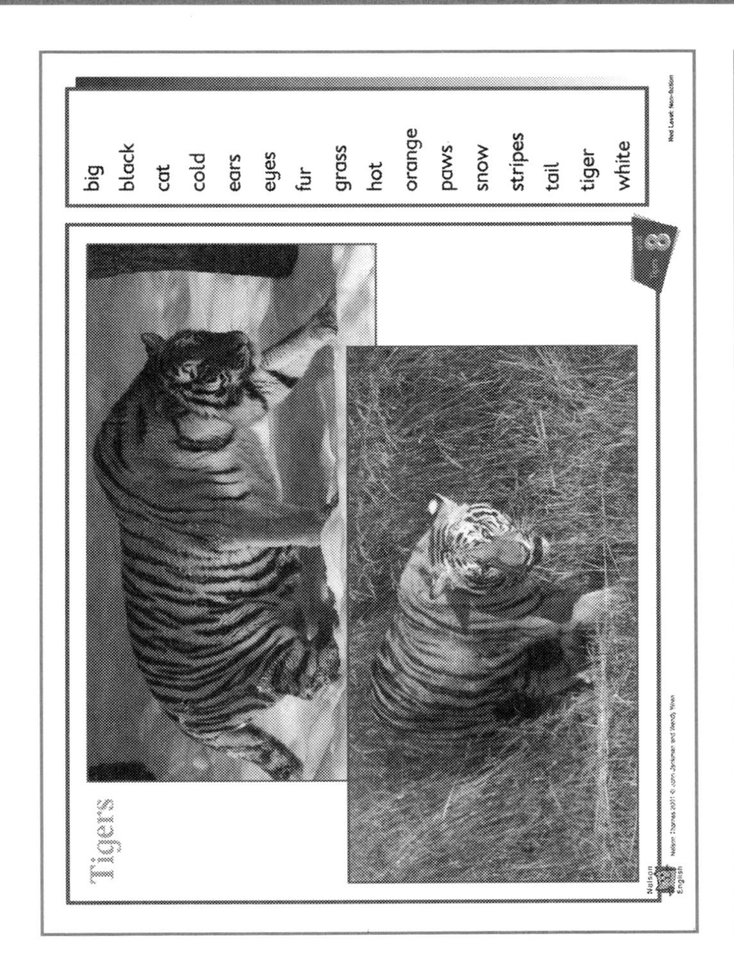

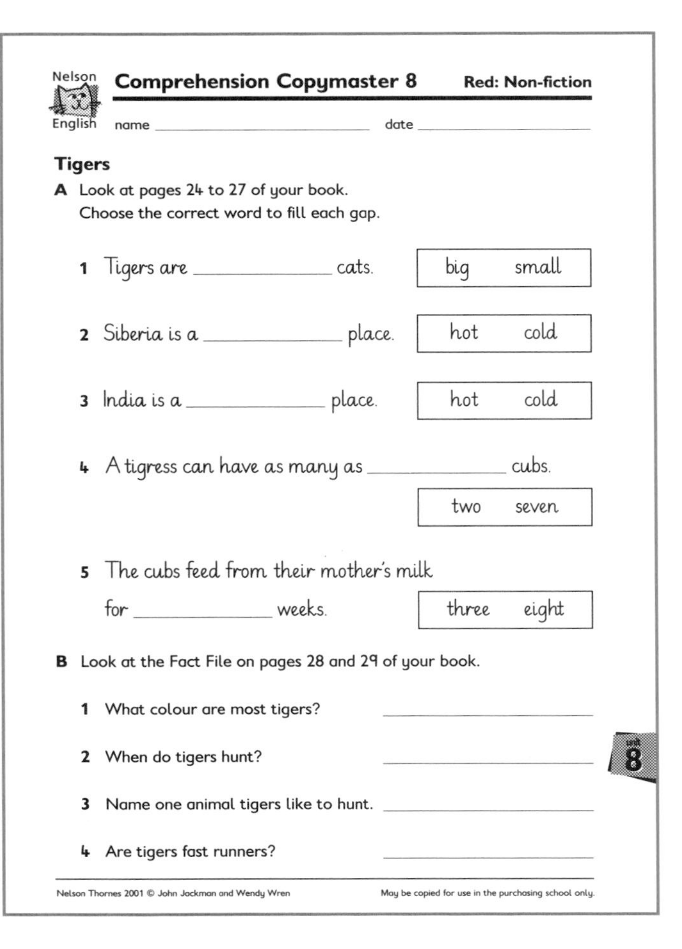

Nelson English **Comprehension Copymaster 8** **Red: Non-fiction**

name ______________________ date ______________________

Tigers

A Look at pages 24 to 27 of your book.
Choose the correct word to fill each gap.

1 Tigers are ____________ cats. | big small |

2 Siberia is a ____________ place. | hot cold |

3 India is a ____________ place. | hot cold |

4 A tigress can have as many as ____________ cubs. | two seven |

5 The cubs feed from their mother's milk for ____________ weeks. | three eight |

B Look at the Fact File on pages 28 and 29 of your book.

1 What colour are most tigers? ____________

2 When do tigers hunt? ____________

3 Name one animal tigers like to hunt. ____________

4 Are tigers fast runners? ____________

Nelson Thornes 2001 © John Jackman and Wendy Wren   May be copied for use in the purchasing school only.

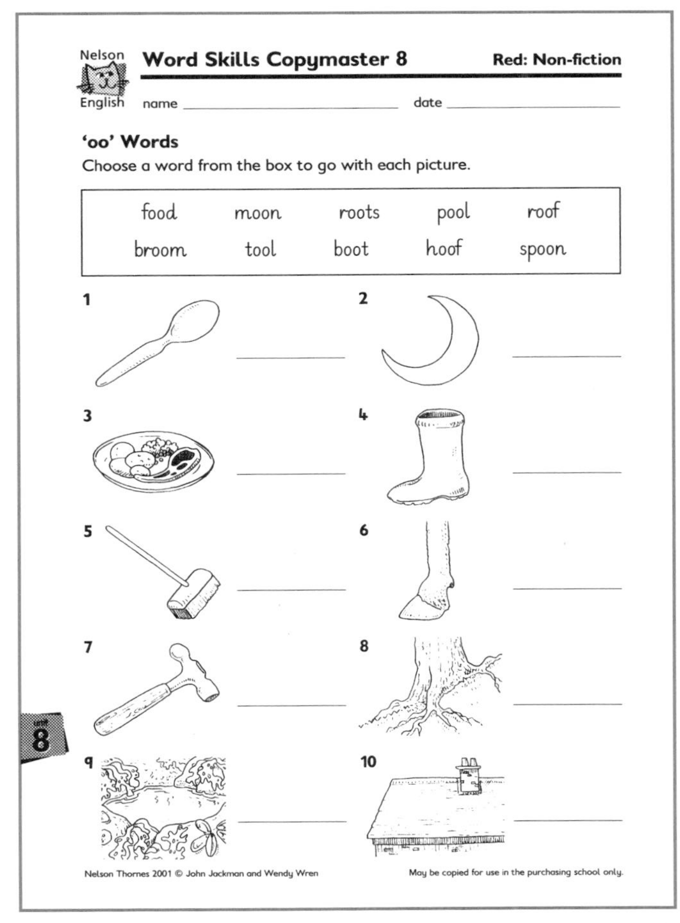

Nelson English **Word Skills Copymaster 8** **Red: Non-fiction**

name ______________________ date ______________________

'oo' Words
Choose a word from the box to go with each picture.

food	moon	roots	pool	roof
broom	tool	boot	hoof	spoon

1 ____________ 2 ____________

3 ____________ 4 ____________

5 ____________ 6 ____________

7 ____________ 8 ____________

9 ____________ 10 ____________

Nelson Thornes 2001 © John Jackman and Wendy Wren   May be copied for use in the purchasing school only.

Nelson English **Writing Copymaster 8** **Red: Non-fiction**

name ______________________ date ______________________

Lions
Look at this picture.

What would you like to find out about lions?
Write your questions here.

Nelson Thornes 2001 © John Jackman and Wendy Wren   May be copied for use in the purchasing school only.

'Who is it?', 'Everybody says' & 'After a Bath'

Fiction

National Literacy Strategy

Year 1 Term 3

Range

Fiction: poems with patterned and predictable structures; a variety of poems on similar themes

Pupils should be taught:

Text level work

Reading comprehension

9 to read a variety of poems on similar themes, e.g. families, school, food;

10 to compare and contrast preferences and common themes in stories and poems;

11 to collect class and individual favourite poems for class anthologies, participate in reading aloud;

Word level work

Phonological awareness, phonics and spelling

1 the common spelling patterns for each of the long vowel phonemes: . . . *ai ie oa* . . . Appendix List 3:

- to identify phonemes in speech and writing; . . .
- to segment words into phonemes for spelling;

Word recognition, graphic knowledge and spelling

4 to read on sight . . . high frequency words identified for Year 1 . . . from Appendix List 1;

Vocabulary extension

9 the terms *'vowel'* and *'consonant'*;

Sentence level work

Grammatical awareness

4 about word order, e.g. by re-ordering sentences, predicting words from previous text, grouping a range of words that might 'fit', and discussing the reasons why;

Sentence construction and punctuation

6 through reading and writing, to reinforce knowledge of the term *sentence* from previous terms;

Text level work

Writing composition

15 to use poems or parts of poems as models for their own writing, e.g. by substituting words or elaborating on the text;

16 to compose own poetic sentences, using repetitive patterns, carefully selected sentences and imagery.

Teaching Notes

Poster: Shared reading

Text level work

The poster shows two simple poems – 'Who is it?' and 'Everybody Says', based on the theme 'Myself'.

Ask the children to follow carefully as you read the poem, pointing to the words as you read.

Read the poem again, asking the children to read along with you.

'Who is it?'

Discuss 'Who is it?' Invite suggestions as to other body parts the poet could have used to build up a picture of herself, for example, arms, eyes, hair, ears, fingers, etc.

Can the children pick out the rhyming words (*nose/toes; see/me*)? Can they think of other words that rhyme with them (for example, *those, goes, hose, rose, shows, owes, pose, flows; we, three, the, free, flee, glee, he, she, knee, pea, sea, tea*)?

This poem lends itself to being memorised and performed with actions, i.e. pointing at the various parts of the body.

'Everybody Says'

Discuss 'Everybody Says'. Prompt with questions such as:

- Who do you think you look like?
- Who do people in your family think you look like?

If some children have bothers or sisters in the school, ask the class whether there is a family resemblance.

Clearly, the family circumstances of children in the class may demand discretion at this point.

Explore the structure of the poem. Can the children identify the rhyming words (*Bee, me*)? Encourage the children to notice that the poem has a different pattern to 'Who is it?' because of the repetition of *Everybody says* and the fact that only the fourth and eighth lines rhyme.

Word level work

This unit provides the opportunity to help children who are capable to identify the three long vowel phonemes – 'ai', 'ie' and 'oa' – in speech and writing and to segment words which incorporate these graphemes for the purpose of spelling.

Remind the group about the five vowel letters and about recent work on modifier (or 'magic') 'e', which makes vowel letters in a word 'say their own name'. Point to the word *nose* in 'Who is it?' on the poster as an example. Ask the children to suggest some other words in which the magic 'e' is operative on the three vowel letters being focussed on (i.e. 'a', 'i', 'o'), e.g. *can/cane; bit/bite; rod/rode.*

As with similar work in earlier units (especially Unit 8 Non-fiction), it is important to gauge the rate at which the different spelling sets can be introduced, so the following is offered primarily as general support and resource material.

Write on the board the simple sentence: *We can't play that game in the rain.* Underline, or write in colour, the three graphemes that represent the long 'a' sound ('ay', 'a-e', 'ai'). Then ask the children to offer other words with the same letter patterns. With the children prompting, write the suggested words in three lists on the board. For example:

'ai' words:

aid	laid	maid	paid	raid		
fail	hail	mail	nail	pail	rail	sail
	tail	wail	frail	trail	snail	
main	pain	rain	Spain			

'-ay' words:

bay	day	hay	jay	lay	may	pay
	ray	say	way			
lay	clay	play				
ray	stay	bray	pray	tray	stray	spray
way	sway					

'a-e' words:

bake	cake	fake	lake	sake	take	flake
	drake	snake	shake			
cave	gave	nave	rave	save	wave	brave
	slave	shave				
came	dame	fame	game	lame	name	same
	tame	flame	frame	shame		

(N.B. *have* is a notable exception.)

Similar activities to those suggested above can be used with the other phonemes.

'oa' words:

oat	boat	coat	goat	moat	float
coal	foal	goal			
foam	roam				
load	road	toad			
loan	moan	groan			
oak	soak	cloak	croak		
boast	coast	roast	toast		
coach	poach	roach			
oak	oat				
load	loaf	loan	soap		

'-y' words:

by	my		
fly	sly		
cry	dry	fry	try
sky	spy	sty	shy

'-igh' words:

high	sigh	thigh				
fight	light	might	night	right	sight	tight
	flight	bright	fright			

For more complete lists, refer to the *Nelson Spelling* Teacher's Book.

As in earlier units and, again, according to ability, two or three words might be selected from the list, and the children asked to illustrate and/or write a sentence including one or more of the words. Also, a cluster of words from the same basic spelling family could be set for the children to learn.

Sentence level work

Poetry is an excellent vehicle for the development of word prediction skills, as it offers the opportunity for auditory discrimination of rhythm and rhyme as well as the application of contextual cues.

The first time the poster is used, cover the last word in each of lines 3 and 4 (*see, ME!*). Explain to the children that the last word in line 3 must rhyme with *toes* (line 1), and similarly the last word in line 4 must rhyme with *see* (line 2).

Play rhyming games by offering simple rhyming couplets for the children to complete, such as:

I banged my head
As I jumped into _____ (bed).

Invite the children to suggest some simple rhymes for the rest of the group to complete.

If appropriate, explain that the way we write poetry is different from 'ordinary' writing (prose), in that each line of a poem usually begins with a capital letter, whereas we do not begin each line with a capital letter in 'normal' writing (this is a common early error). Use the opportunity to consider again the difference between a line of text and a sentence. The children might also spot that many lines in poems end with a comma – another way it differs from prose.

Pupil's book

Text level work

Introduction

The pupil's book continues the theme of 'Myself' with the poem 'After a Bath', which describes the common experience of having a bath. Like 'Who is it?', the poem features parts of the body.

Read the poem with the children and prompt an immediate response as to whether they like the poem or not. Allow the discussion to expand into talking about the children's own experiences of bath time.

Base a discussion on the following points to establish literal understanding.
- What does the poet do after she has a bath?
- What does she have to dry?
- What does she wish she could do?

Give the children the opportunity to:
- recite the poem
- recite the poem and do the actions
- pick out the rhyming words (*try/dry, toes/nose, take/shake*).

If time allows, let children explore simple poetry anthologies to find other poems on a similar theme.

Reading comprehension

Comprehension Copymaster 9 Fiction requires the children to pick out literal information from the poem in the pupil's book, and to draw and write about their own experience of bath time. This could include getting into the bath, playing/washing/hair-washing in the bath, etc. The writing will vary from a simple caption to several sentences, depending on individual ability. The comprehension questions in section A can be approached as a class discussion, in guided or independently working groups, or individually.

Word level work

'a-e', 'ai', 'ay', 'igh' and 'y' words

Word Skills Copymaster 9 Fiction continues the work on 'a-e', 'ai' and 'ay' vowel digraphs.

Write the following words on the board.

night	cry	high	fight	light	sigh	thigh
try	shy	tight	fly	right	sly	

The words can then be sorted according to their 'rime' patterns. Divide the rest of the board into three columns under the headings: *'-y' words, '-igh' words* and *'-ight' words*. Invite children to sort the words under the correct headings, either by copying the headings and writing each word under the correct heading, or by coming forward and writing one word at a time under the correct heading on the board.

The high-frequency words for this unit, to be taught as 'sight recognition' words, are as follows.

Monday
Tuesday
Wednesday
Thursday
Friday

Sentence level work

Poetry and prose

Use the poem to reinforce the notion that a line of text and a sentence are different, and that different punctuation conventions apply.

Continue with group and individual activities in which the children finish and illustrate rhyming couplets. This will lead naturally into the Text level work.

Text level work

Writing composition

Following on from the poster/pupil's book discussion, the children should write their own poems using 'After a Bath' as the model. For children who need support, **Writing Copymaster 9 Fiction** provides lists of suitable rhyming words which they can make use of in their writing, and ruled lines showing the structure of the poem. Some children will only manage a rhyming couplet, others may achieve a four-line verse. Use the copymaster in class/group discussion, adding other words where possible. Be on hand to help individuals with their writing and have a plenary session in which the children can read their poems to the class.

Copymaster answers

Comprehension Copymaster 9

A 1 dry
2 *Any two of the following:* hands, fingers, toes, legs, nose
3 nose
4 She would like to shake herself like a dog.
5 It would be quicker.

B *Individual answers.*

Word Skills Copymaster 9

A *Children say and copy the words.*

B 1 snail 2 cake 3 lake
4 spray 5 tray 6 tail

Writing Copymaster 9

Individual answers.

Who is it?

Take …
A head, some shoulders, knees and toes,
A mouth and eyes that see,
A pair of legs, two feet, one nose,
And what you've got is
ME!

Everybody says

Everybody says
I look just like my mother.
Everybody says
I'm the image of Aunt Bee.
Everybody says
My nose is like my father's
But *I* want to look like
ME!

Red Level: Fiction

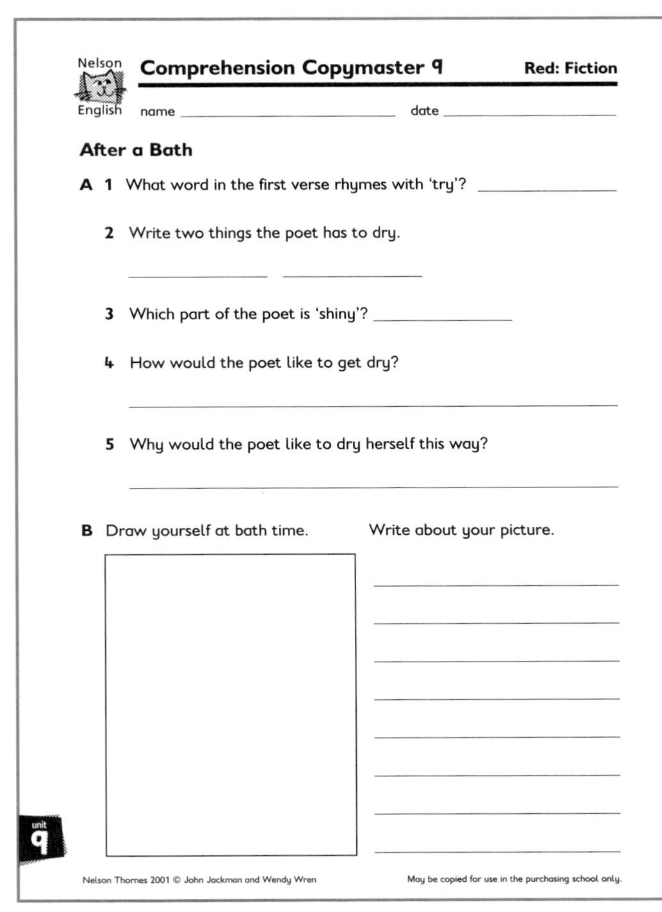

Nelson English **Comprehension Copymaster 9** **Red: Fiction**

name ______________________ date ______________________

After a Bath

A **1** What word in the first verse rhymes with 'try'? ______________

2 Write two things the poet has to dry.

______________ ______________

3 Which part of the poet is 'shiny'? ______________

4 How would the poet like to get dry?

____

5 Why would the poet like to dry herself this way?

____

B Draw yourself at bath time. Write about your picture.

unit 9

Nelson English **Word Skills Copymaster 9** **Red: Fiction**

name ______________________ date ______________________

Matching Words

A Say each word out loud. Copy each word.

game	tame	lay
play	rain	train

B Choose a word from the box to go with each picture.

tray	cake	tail	spray	lake	snail

1 2 3

4 5 6

unit 9

Nelson English **Writing Copymaster 9** **Red: Fiction**

name ______________________ date ______________________

Having a Bath

bubble trouble	rub tub	squiggle wriggle giggle	cry eye dry my
soap hope grope	wet get let		

unit 9

unit 9

My Body & Growing up

Non-fiction

National Literacy Strategy

Year 1 Term 3

Range

Non-fiction: information texts . . .

Pupils should be taught:

Text level work

Reading comprehension

17 to identify simple questions and use text to find answers. To locate parts of text that give particular information including labelled diagrams and charts . . .

Word level work

Word recognition, graphic knowledge and spelling

4 to read on sight . . . high frequency words identified for Year 1 . . . from Appendix List 1;

6 to investigate and learn the spelling of verbs with 'ed' (past tense), 'ing' (present tense) endings;

Sentence level work

Sentence construction and punctuation

5 other common uses of capitalisation, e.g. for personal titles (*Mr*, *Miss*), headings, book titles, emphasis;

7 to add question marks to questions;

Text level work

Writing composition

21 to use the language and features of non-fiction texts, e.g. labelled diagrams, captions for pictures, to make class books . . .

Teaching Notes

Poster: Shared reading

Text level work

Revise earlier work on the difference between fiction and non-fiction (Units 5 and 8 Non-fiction). Remind the children that a non-fiction book gives us information.

Display the poster and ask the children to explain what they can see. Remind the children of the work they did in Unit 7 Non-fiction and ask them how this information is presented, i.e. labelled diagram.

Read through the vocabulary strip, explaining that the words can be used to describe people. Ask the children how the words in the vocabulary strip are organised (i.e. alphabetically).

Ask the children for sentences which describe the girl, e.g. *The girl has long hair.* Ask some of the children to describe themselves.

Word level work

Remind the children that when we are talking or writing about something which is happening now – in the present – we usually add 'ing' to the action word. Acting as scribe, ask the children to tell you what is happening in the classroom, using a sentence that contains a present-tense action word with the 'ing' suffix, e.g. *We are reading the poster.* Remind the group of some of the 'ing' words that the class collected when working on Unit 8 Fiction.

Remind the children that, if we are writing about something which has already happened, we usually add 'ed' or 'd' to the action word instead of 'ing'. Give an example, such as *talk – talking – talked.*

Invite the children to use 'ed' words to describe what they have already done earlier in the day, e.g. *jumped out of bed, washed my face, walked to school, played with X, listened to the teacher, talked to Y*, etc. Acting as scribe, record these on the board, pointing out how often the action word finishes with 'ed'.

Sentence level work

Once again, go over the essential components of a sentence – that it makes sense, that it begins with a capital letter and ends with a full stop. Ask a volunteer to suggest a sentence about the picture on the poster, e.g. *The girl is wearing green shorts.* Write the sentence on the board, and discuss whether and why it is a sentence.

Write on the board a question that relates to the picture on the poster, e.g. *What colour is her hair?* Consider whether this is a sentence. Work through each of the sentence criteria. When you come to the need for a full stop you may need to remind the class that the question mark has a built-in full stop, so is also a suitable end to a sentence.

Ask the children to suggest other questions about the poster illustration. Write them on the board and, when you have collected three or four sentences, ask selected children to come forward in turn and circle one of the question marks.

Pupil's book

Text level work

Introduction

Following on from the poster, the pupil's book contains a pictorial timeline of the stages of human growth.

Look at each photograph in turn and ask the children how old they think the person/people shown are.

Alternatively, ask a series of questions so that the children have to locate the information, e.g.:

- Which photograph shows the youngest person?
- Which photograph shows the oldest person?
- Which photograph do you think shows someone of about your age?
- Which photograph shows a younger child? Which photograph shows an older child? etc.

This activity can be done in writing, using **Comprehension Copymaster 9 Non-fiction**.

Point out to the children that both the poster and the pupil's book give us information. Ask how the two ways in which it is presented are the same (i.e. both use pictures) and in which it is different (i.e. the poster has labels; the order of the photos in the pupil's book is important).

Reading comprehension

Comprehension Copymaster 9 Non-fiction requires the children to answer questions about the photographs in the pupil's book. The comprehension questions can be approached as a class discussion, in guided or independently working groups, or individually.

Word level work

Past-tense verbs

Use **Word Skills Copymaster 9 Non-fiction** for practice in adding 'ing' and 'ed' to action words (verbs).

Ask the children to offer sentences that include an 'ed' verb. Stress that 'ed' verbs only appear in sentences about events that have happened in the past (i.e. past tense).

Collect and write, with the children copying, some other 'ed' or 'd' verbs. Ask the children to try to write a sentence using one of these past-tense action words.

The high-frequency words for this unit, to be taught as 'sight recognition' words, are as follows.

Saturday
Sunday
brown
pink
white

Sentence level work

Questions

Question marks are not an easy shape to master, so ensure that the children have sufficient practice and draw attention to the full stop at the foot of each. Part B of **Word Skills Copymaster 9 Non-fiction** requires children to practice writing question marks.

Recap on the work done in Unit 8 Fiction covering the use of capital letters for titles (e.g. *Mr, Ms,* etc). Ask the children to write the full names, with titles, of five adults, such as family members, teachers or neighbours.

Text level work

Writing composition

Each child should draw a picture of himself/herself and label it. Display the poster so that the children can use the vocabulary strip for reference. Encourage them to add descriptive detail such as: *small hands, round face*, etc.

For children who need support with this activity, **Writing Copymaster 9 Non-fiction** provides an outline drawing with space to write labels.

If possible, ask each child to bring in a photograph of himself/herself which does not have to be returned. Stick each photograph to a separate piece of paper and help each child to write a short description of themself. They can include likes/dislikes, special skills, etc. if they wish.

Collect the labelled pictures and photograph sheets together in a class book called 'Ourselves'. Allow a double-page spread, for each child, with their labelled drawing on the left-hand page and the photograph and written description on the right-hand page.

Copymaster answers

Comprehension Copymaster 9

1 photo 2
2 photo 9
3 photo 4
4 photos 2 and 3
5 photo 5
6 *Probably* photo 6 *or* 7

Word Level Copymaster 9

A *Children complete the words by adding 'ing' and 'ed'.*

B 1 Who walked to school this morning?
2 Has your brother mended your bike yet?
3 Who watched television last night?
4 Are you waiting for the next bus?
5 Is Dad cooking our tea tonight?

Writing Copymaster 9

Individual answers.

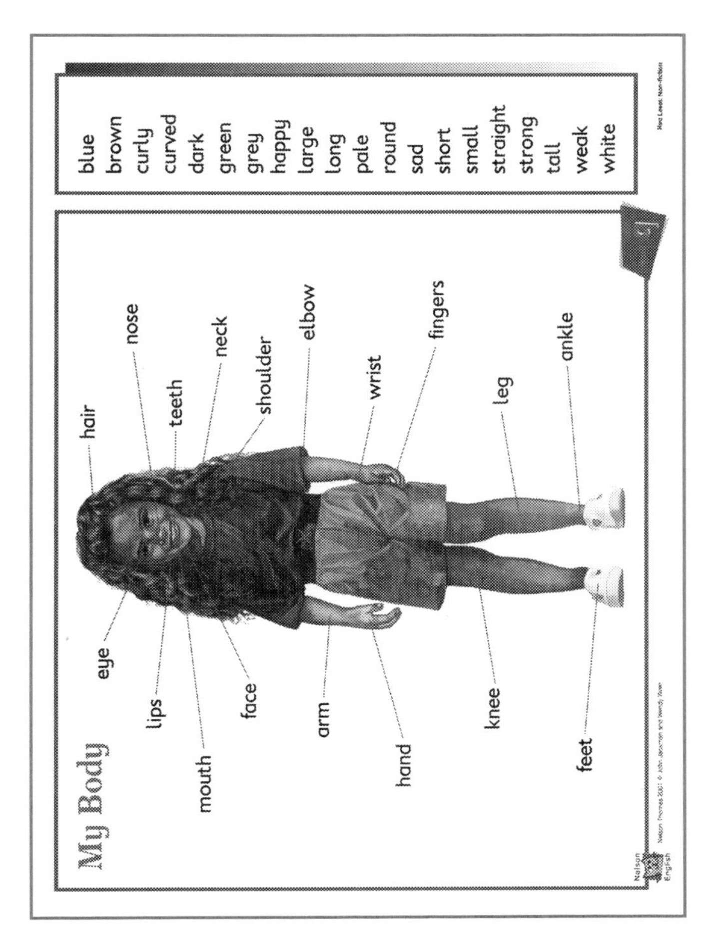

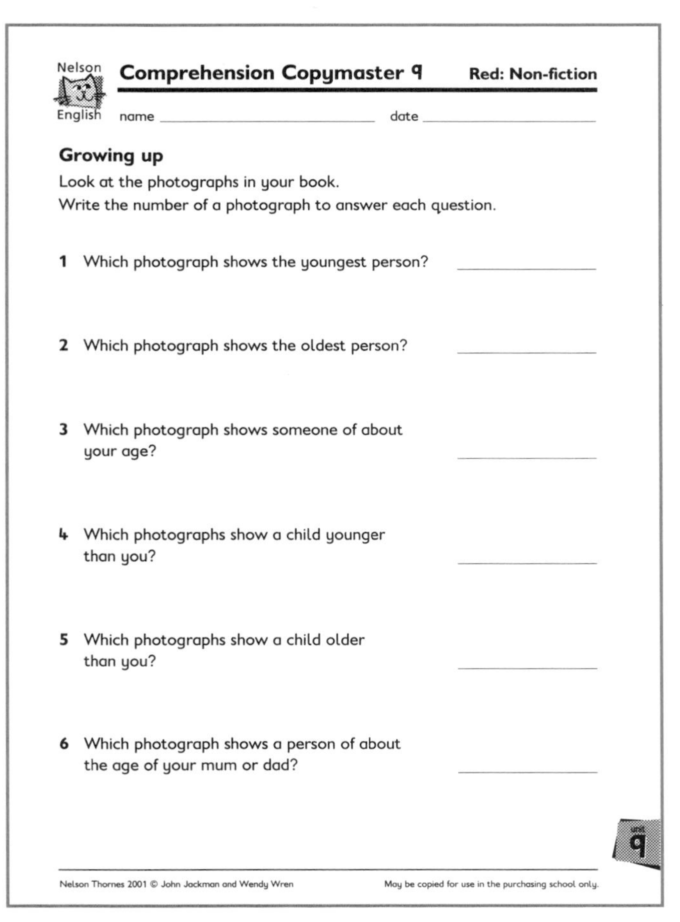

Nelson English **Comprehension Copymaster 9** **Red: Non-fiction**

name ______________________ date ______________

Growing up

Look at the photographs in your book.
Write the number of a photograph to answer each question.

1 Which photograph shows the youngest person? ________

2 Which photograph shows the oldest person? ________

3 Which photograph shows someone of about your age? ________

4 Which photographs show a child younger than you? ________

5 Which photographs show a child older than you? ________

6 Which photograph shows a person of about the age of your mum or dad? ________

unit 9

Nelson English **Word Skills Copymaster 9** **Red: Non-fiction**

name ______________________ date ______________

Action Words

A Finish these word sums.

1 walk + ing = ________ 2 walk + ed = ________

3 talk + ing = ________ 4 talk + ed = ________

5 jump + ing = ________ 6 jump + ed = ________

7 mend + ing = ________ 8 mend + ed = ________

9 watch + ing = ________ 10 watch + ed = ________

11 wait + ing = ________ 12 wait + ed = ________

13 cook + ing = ________ 14 cook + ed = ________

B Use the words you made in part A to help you fill the gaps.
Add a question mark to finish each question.

1 Who ________ to school this morning ___

2 Has your brother ________ your bike yet ___

3 Who ________ television last night ___

4 Are you ________ for the next bus ___

5 Is Dad ________ our tea tonight ___

unit 9

Nelson English **Writing Copymaster 9** **Red: Non-fiction**

name ______________________ date ______________

My Body

Draw on this outline and colour it so it looks like you.
Add labels with arrows to describe how you look.

unit 9

Nelson English Key Stage 2

BOOK 1
7-8 YEARS

Developing Fiction Skills
Book 1
0-17-424732-X

Developing Non-fiction
Skills Book 1
0-17-424731-1

Teacher's Guide
Book 1
0-17-424734-6

Copymaster Resource
Book 1
0-17-424741-9

BOOK 2
8-9 YEARS

Developing Fiction Skills
Book 2
0-17-424750-8

Developing Non-fiction
Skills Book 2
0-17-424751-6

Teacher's Guide
Book 2
0-17-424743-5

Copymaster Resource
Book 2
0-17-424752-4

BOOK 3
9-10 YEARS

Developing Fiction Skills
Book 3
0-17-424755-9

Developing Non-fiction
Skills Book 3
0-17-424756-7

Teacher's Guide
Book 3
0-17-424757-5

Copymaster Resource
Book 3
0-17-424753-2

BOOK 4
10-11 YEARS

Developing Fiction Skills
Book 4
0-17-424773-7

Developing Non-fiction
Skills Book 4
0-17-424774-5

Teacher's Guide
Book 4
0-17-424772-9

Copymaster Resource
Book 4
0-17-424754-0